Wiley Jones

The Gospel of the Kingdom

Wiley Jones

The Gospel of the Kingdom

ISBN/EAN: 9783337184070

Printed in Europe, USA, Canada, Australia, Japan

Cover: Foto ©Lupo / pixelio.de

More available books at **www.hansebooks.com**

THE GOSPEL OF THE KINGDOM,

ADVOCATED IN A SERIES OF

TEN DISCOURSES.

BY
WILEY JONES,
NORFOLK, VA.

The Preaching of Christ:—"Now after that John was put in prison, Jesus came into Galilee preaching the gospel of the kingdom of God."—MARK I, 14.

The Preaching of His Apostles:—"This gospel of the kingdom shall be preached in all the world."—MAT. XXIV, 14; AC. I, 8; COL. I, 6, 23.

The Apostolic warning:—"Though we, or an angel from heaven, preach *any other* gospel unto you than that which we have preached unto you, let him be accursed."—GAL. I, 8, 9.

The Apostolic exhortation;—"Earnestly contend for the faith which was once delivered unto the saints."—JUDE 3.

VIRGINIAN STEAM PRESSES,
NORFOLK, VA.
1879:

PREFACE.

These discourses are not *verbatim* reports, but were written out principally from *short notes* used in speaking. The subjects, as will be seen, are of the utmost importance, embracing the leading points of "The faith of the gospel."

This volume is now sent on its travels with the humble and fervent prayer that, under the blessing of the Lord, it may assist many in obtaining a knowledge of that Gospel which "is the power of God unto salvation to every one that believeth."

Norfolk, March, 1879.

FIRST DISCOURSE.

HOW TO STUDY THE BIBLE.

"Search the Scriptures."—John v, 39. "They received the word with all readiness of mind, and searched the Scriptures daily, whether those things were so. Therefore many of them believed."—Ac. xvii, 11, 12.

1. We should study the Bible with *delight*. The holy writers, although endowed with inspiration themselves, used to take delight in studying the written word. Thus Paul, "I delight in the law of God."—Rom. vii, 22. And the Psalmist, "How sweet are thy words unto my taste! Yea, sweeter than honey to my mouth! O how I love thy law! it is my meditation all the day."—Psa. cxix, 97, 103. "Blessed is the man whose delight is in the law of the Lord."—Psa. i, 2. And even the Great Redeemer himself read the Holy Scriptures; it was "His *custom*."—Lu. iv, 16. Why then should not *we* delight in the study of that sacred volume? It is commended to us as an "*able*" word,—"*able* to make thee wise unto salvation through faith which is in Christ Jesus . . . *able* to build thee up, and to give thee an inheritance among all them which are sanctified."

2 Tim. iii, 16: Ac. xx, 32. All through life it is a lamp to our feet and a guide to our steps—"Thou shalt guide me by thy counsel, and afterwards receive me to glory."—Psa. lxxiii, 24. In earliest youth it comes to us with the timely exhortation, "Remember *now* thy Creator, in the days of thy *youth*."—Eccles. xii, 1. In the feverish battle of life it gives many a cooling sip of "precious promises," and, like a ministering angel, at the dying hour it softly whispers, "underneath are the everlasting arms . . . Yea, though I walk through the valley of the shadow of death I will fear no evil, for thy rod and thy staff they comfort me."

That the Bible is one of the greatest blessings bestowed on mankind is generally acknowledged by all who have taken the pains to acquaint themselves with the value and worth of it. I once heard a pious and learned young Christian say, "The more I study the Bible, the more I want to study it." A celebrated scholar and linguist has said, "I have regularly and attentively read the Holy Scriptures, and am of the opinion that this volume contains more true sublimity, more exquisite beauty, more pure morality, more important history, and finer strains both of poetry and eloquence, than could be collected from all other books." In what light soever we read the Bible, whether with reference to revelation, to history, or to morality, it is an invaluable and inexhaustible mine of knowledge and virtue. But we cannot briefly enumerate its countless benefits; and therefore, with these few seed-thoughts on its preciousness, I pass to a second branch of the subject

2. We should study the Bible with child-like *submission* to its dictates. The Bible is the sovereign test in all matters, whether of faith or practice. "To the law and to the testimony; if they speak not according to this word, it is because there is no light in them."—Isa. viii, 20. "Prove all things, hold fast that which is good."—1 Thes. v, 21. An authoritative message has been sent from the throne of God, and therefore the formation of our religious creed is no longer left to the dreams of imagination, or the speculations of philosophy; but it is to be deduced fairly and honestly from the written record alone. The apostles wrought real and true miracles in confirmation of what they said; and yet the Bereans examined even their teachings by the test of scripture,—they "searched the scriptures daily, whether those things were so. Therefore many of them believed." And they were commended as " noble," for their conduct. How much more necessary then is it for us to examine what we hear (no matter *who* may say it), and to have a "Thus saith the Lord" or a "Thus it is written" for every article of our faith and practice!*

---

* "Holy Scripture containeth all things necessary to salvation; so that whatever is not read therein, nor may be

But many believers of error pride themselves on the witness of their own heart, or the teaching of the spirit within them, as they call it. They ought to remember however that the Spirit of God in the heart would not in one jot or tittle contradict the Spirit of God in the Bible, for the Spirit of God nowhere contradicts the word of God. When Paul said, "The Spirit beareth witness with our spirit, that we are the children of God" he was speaking of himself and those early disciples who, like him, had believed the *gospel of the kingdom,* and also had been *immersed "for the remission of sins."* But I once heard a man who had neither believed that gospel nor received that immersion apply this language to himself, as proof of his being a Christian; but this was a glaring misapplication and perversion of that scripture. The feelings of the heart are never to be trusted where they conflict with the written word, for "The heart is deceitful above all things, and des-

proved thereby, is not to be required of any man, that it should be believed as an article of faith, or be thought requisite or necessary to salvation,"—Episcopal Creed, Art. VI.

☞ I have occasionally quoted uninspired writers not as authority or proof, but for the sake of some truth which they have expressed in a forcible manner. Paul himself (who tells us to do what we have seen and heard in him, Phil. iv, 9) sometimes with good effect, quoted even heathen poets when they chanced to say some valuable *truth*; but not as authority or proof, nor as endorsing any of their *untrue* sayings. Ac. xvii, 28; Titus i, 12.

perately wicked."—Jer. xvii, 9. "Out of the heart proceed evil thoughts."—Mat. xv, 19. Hence the Scripture has also said, "He that trusteth in his own heart is a fool."—Prov. xxviii, 6. Saul and others "verily thought" that they were doing God service when they were "making havoc of the church" by cruel persecutions, but did their sincerity turn their crime into a virtue? Jno. xvi, 2: Ac. xxvi, 9–11. Sincerity will not render harmless the believing of error any more than it will the drinking of poison. The modern theory of sincerity, is not found in the Bible. Its advocates tell us that even idolaters will be saved, if they are sincere, and live up to the light they have. But the Bible declares that "idolaters shall have their part in the lake of fire and brimstone, which is the second death."—Rev. xxi, 8. It speaks of the philosophical Greek idolaters of Ephesus (Ac. xix, 35,) as "without Christ, having *no hope*, and without God in the world . . . Being *aleniated* from the life of God through the *ignorance* that was in them."—Ephes. ii, 12: iv, 18. And Paul did not preach to them that modern gospel of sincerity (which is a delusion and a snare), but faithfully declared to them "the gospel of *the kingdom*," as the Master had commanded.—Mat. xxiv, 14: Ac. xx, 25. If every man's own sincerity of heart were to be made the standard and evidence of what is right would not all the various and conflicting sects of Protestantism, Catholicism and

Paganism have an equal claim to be right? for I suppose they all claim to be *sincere*, and to have some sort of an approving witness in their own hearts. They need to be warned however that "there is a way which seemeth right unto a man, but the end thereof are the ways of death."—Prov. xiv, 12.

We see then the absolute necessity of submitting entirely and without reserve to the dictates of the word of God which he has "magnified above all His name."—Psa. cxxxviii, 2. His word enlightens,—"The entrance of thy word giveth light" (Psa. cxix, 130): corrects,—"Through thy precepts I get understanding; therefore I hate every *false* way" (Psa. cxix, 104): converts,—"The law of the Lord is perfect, converting the soul," (Psa. xix, 7): and shields from sin,—"Thy word have I hid in my heart, that I might not sin against thee."—Psa. cxix, 11.

3. Heeding the "sure word of *prophecy*." In order that our faith may be "built upon the foundation of the apostles and prophets, Jesus Christ himself being the chief corner stone" we should study the *whole* Bible, and not merely that part which was written by the apostles. The same God speaks to us through both, and the same "Spirit of Christ" which inspired the apostles inspired the prophets also.—1 Pet. i, 11: Ephes. ii, 20. These two classes of testimony—prophetic and apostolic—may be called the two sources from which "as new

born babes" we derive "the sincere milk of the word" in our earliest perceptions of saving truth— 1 Pet. ii, 2. They may be compared to the two wings on which in growing strength we mount up as eagles.—Isa. xl, 30. We may liken them to the two edges of that "sword of the spirit which is the word of God," and which "a good soldier of Jesus Christ," wields to the conviction and conversion of others.—Eph. vi, 17: 2 Tim. ii, 3.

When the Saviour said "Search the Scriptures," that portion of the Bible called the New Testament had not been written. Hence neglecting the study of the prophets would be neglecting this command of the Saviour. The apostles likewise require us to "be mindful, (i. e. 'regardful, attentive, observant,'—Webster) of the words which were spoken before by the holy prophets," and they declare that in taking *heed* to the word of prophecy we "*do well.*" It is a "light" which we dare not hide under a bushel. 2 Pet. i, 19: iii, 2. Take warning by Israel of old, and the things that "happened unto them for examples; and are written for our admonition." 1 Cor. x, 11. Why was that nation made "a curse, an astonishment, a hissing and a reproach among all the nations?" "Because they hearkened not to my words, saith the Lord, which I sent unto them by my servants the prophets." Jer. xxix, 17–19. Behold what a value the Saviour has attached to the prophets, and to the convincing power of their testimony—"If they hear not Moses and the prophets, neither will they be persuaded though one rose from the dead." Lev. xvi, 31. And again, "*All* things must be fulfilled which are written in the law of Moses, in the prophets and in the Psalms concerning me."—Lu. xxiv, 44. Their great themes ought to command the devout attention of every one who truly loves the Saviour, for they speak of "the sufferings of Christ and the glory that should follow," or, more accurately translated, "the sufferings destined for Christ, and the glories after these."—1 Pet. i, 11. The glories include His resurrection, His ascension His intercession above, His future return " with power and great glory" to take His seat on "the throne of His glory" (Mat xxiv, 30: xxv, 31,) to "reign in mount Zion and in Jerusalem, before His ancients gloriously" (Isa. xxiii, 24), and finally to fill the whole earth with His glory.—Num. xiv, 21.*

And why object to the study of unfulfilled

---

* "Prophecy serves as the basis of our hope in the things yet to come, in the final triumph of truth and righteousness on earth, the universal establishment of the kingdom of our Lord, and in the rewards of eternal life to be bestowed at His 2nd appearing,"—Edwards' Encyclopedia. "Prophecy is interwoven with every part of the Bible from Genesis to the Revelation."—The Mine Explored, by the American Sunday School Union, "The subject of prophecy makes so large a proportion of Scripture, that no one can slight it without disobeying the plain direction of Searching the Scriptures"—Comprehensive Commentary.

prophecy? By believing and heeding what was as yet an unfulfilled prophecy, Noah "prepared an ark to the saving of his house; by the which he condemned the world, and became heir of the righteousness which is by faith."—Heb. xi, 7. And is it not perfectly fair to infer that if, under any pretext whatever, he had neglected or ignored that prophecy he would have perished along with the rest? as did also the sons-in-law of Lot for neglecting unfulfilled prophecy.—Gen. xix, 14. No doubt they regarded Lot as *"an alarmist."* Perhaps real estate was higher in Sodom the day before than it had been for years, inducing the so-called "smart, shrewd, business men" of the place to rush into the market greedily buying for a still further rise. Planting too was going on, and perhaps the suburban farmers were expecting large crops and great gains, for it was a fertile valley.— Lu. xvii, 28.

I tremble for those who confine their studies entirely to the fulfilled prophecies. What! does the word of God need to be confirmed by historical events before you deem it worthy of study or belief? A true worshipper should, like Paul, believe not only the fulfilled things but *"all* things which are written in the law and in the prophets."— Ac. xxiv, 14. What are all those precious promises of the gospel which hold out to us the hope of the second coming of Christ, the resurrection morn, and all the joys of an endless life but unfulfilled prophecies? To cast aside all such prophecies, therefore, would blow out the light of the believer's animating hope, and leave us in the deadly darkness of utter despair. We are commanded to hear Christ "in *all* things whatsoever."—(Ac. iii, 22), and one of His longest recorded discourses is a series of prophecies, which, to be clearly understood, must be compared with *other* prophecies.— Mat. xxiv and xxv. The last book of the Bible is a christian prophecy, and was sent to the early churches with a *blessing* twice pronounced on those who read, hear, and keep "those things which are written therein."—Rev. 1, 3: xxii, 7. And was this blessing pronounced on the study of it because it had become a fulfilled prophecy? No, but because it was unfulfilled. The reason is given in these words, "*For* the time is *at hand*."—Rev. i, 3. This promise of a blesssing ought to be a sufficient inducement to the study of that prophecy, and the study of *that* necessitates and opens the door to the study of Daniel, Zechariah, Ezekiel, &c., all of them serving, when compared, to more clearly explain one another.

What if some have erred and advanced wild theories on the unfulfilled phophecies, should this prevent us from searching for their true meaning? There have been quacks in the medical profession, but does that prevent people from taking medicine when they are sick? On what point of Christian doctrine have errors and wild theories not been promulgated? On the very origin and creation of man we have heard in our day of a sect of mad philosophers advocating the sheerest nonsense. On the remission of sins, on baptism, the Lord's Supper, the resurrection, and on many other subjects there have been wild theories of error started in the world by those who wrest the Scriptures to their own destruction.—2 Peter iii, 16. But shall these perverters make us relinquish the real teaching of the Bible on those subjects? No, not for a moment.

4. Comparing Scripture with Scripture. All the plain texts, from Genesis to Revelation, relating to any particular subject, must be taken together impartially compared, and the expressions of one of them restricted by those of another, and explained in mutual consistency. Then, the doctrine fairly deduced from them all in conjunction is the doctrine of the Bible on that particular subject. We are not to expect in every place the whole circle of Christian truth to be fully stated: and therefore no conclusion should be drawn from the absence of a doctrine from one passage so long as we can find that doctrine clearly stated in another.

This is a rule of common sense, and is so just and so essential to a right understanding of the Bible, or indeed of any other book, that I wonder it is not observed by all. And yet in a vast number of instances it is neglected, sometimes through mere indolence, and sometimes through a desire to deceive others. The neglect of it, however, is a fruitful source of crude notions, false doctrines, and destructive heresies, of nearly every shade and degree. For example, the Roman Catholics quote, "This is my body," and detaching this from similar texts that would explain it, they tell us that the bread and wine are so changed as to contain "the body, soul and divinity" of Christ. And this monstrous falsehood leads them to another sin —that of idolatry—for they pay divine honors to a piece of dough that has been baked over a fire. Does this idolatry differ in degree of guilt from the ancient worship of a piece of wood cut from a tree? —Isa. xliv, 13-20. And yet millions of Protestants have been bitterly and cruelly persecuted by Romanists for not joining in such a blasphemous perversion of this text. If you should protest to the Romanist, " I *see* that it is a wafer, it *tastes* like a wafer, it *smells* like a wafer, to the *touch* it crumbles like a wafer of flour and water, to the *hearing* it sounds like a wafer, if I let it fall, and if I leave it long enough it corrupts and moulders like a wafer," his answer is, " Your five senses deceive you."

But all of the five divinely-given senses testify that it is not changed, but is still a wafer; while only one of those senses, (the eyesight), testifies that the words, "This is my body," are in the Book at all. Would it be any more absurb to say that *one* of my senses deceives me with reference to those words, than to say that *all* of them deceive me with reference to the wafer? But what need of arguing when we can learn, by merely comparing other portions of Scripture, that it is only a symbol, and that even in the act of eating, it still remains *bread* —"as often as ye eat this *bread*." Three times in as many consecutive verses, the substance eaten is declared to be bread.—1 Cor. xi, 26, 27, 28. And as to the cup, we are forbidden to partake of blood, but commanded to partake of the wine. Therefore. the wine is not blood but only an *emblem* of it.— Gen. ix, 4: Lev. xvii, 14: Ac. xv, 29, Mat. xxvi, 27. When the Saviour says,, 'I am the door," or "I am the vine," we are not to pervert his words and say that he is changed into a literal piece of carpenter's work, or a literal vine. And so the words "This is my body," mean only that the broken bread represents his body. Compare further, many similar expressions, as "Behold the Lamb of God."—Jno. i, 36. "That rock was Christ."—1 Cor. x, 4. "The seven ears of corn are seven years."—Gen. xli, 26. "The seven candlesticks are seven churches."—Rev. i, 20. "The seven heads are seven mountains."—Rev. xvii, 9. "Their throat is an open sepulchre."—Rom. iii, 13. "Thou art that head of gold," and so on.—Dan. ii, 38. If I take you into a school room, and pointing to a map on the wall, say "This is America," "That is Europe," "That is Asia," you never suppose the canvas and paint are transubstantiated into America, Europe, or Asia.*

But many Protestants also violate this rule in matters of the utmost importance. For instance; the three following truths which, as great first priciples, every person in the world ought to be acquainted with, are clearly taught in the Bible.

1. That "THE GOSPEL OF THE KINGDOM" is what the Lord Jesus preached in Palestine during all His personal ministry. The proof of this is too clear to be denied. "Jesus went about all the cities and villages teaching in their synagogues, and preaching the gospel of *the kingdom.*" —Mat. ix, 35, iv, 23. "He went throughout every city and viliage, preaching and showing the glad tidings of *the kingdom of God.*"—Lu. viii, 1. And in the sacred interval between His resurrection and ascension He conversed with His disciples, "being seen of them forty days, and speaking of the things pertaining to *the kingdom of God;*" the earliest and the latest theme of His teaching on earth.—Ac. i, 3.

2. "THIS GOSPEL OF THE KINGDOM" is what the apostles went forth and preached

---

* Notice the case of Balaam as another illustration of comparing Scripture to gain all the evidence on any point. We find his general history in Numbers xxii, &c.; his *motive* in 2 Pet. ii, 15; how *deeply* seated was his covetousness, in Jude 11; that it was at *his* instigation Balak threw that temptation in the way of the Israelites, in Rev. ii, 14.

in all the world after He ascended They did this by express directions of the Master who towards the close of His own personal ministry said to them, by way of prediction and command, "This gospel of the kingdom shall be preached in all the world." —Mat. xxiv, 14. Any tolerably bright youth in a Sunday school ought to be able to tell you that the Saviour's own personal ministry was confined to the land of Palestine. By whom, then, was it preached in all the world? Certainly not by the hostile Scribes and Pharisees, nor the sneering Gentile philosophers. It must therefore have been preached by the Apostles, for it was they whom the Master appointed to that work, saying, "Go *ye* into all the world and preach the gospel to every creature."—Mar. xvi, 15. "*Ye* shall be witnesses unto me both in Jerusalem, and in all Judea, and in Samaria, and unto the uttermost part of the earth."—Ac. i, 8. And though dead we may say that they are still preaching it in *their writings* (but not in their self-styled "successors"), wherever the Bible is read, or translated into a new dialect by the noble Bible Societies. The words of the Master—"This gospel of the kingdom shall be preached in all the world"—are plain enough proof that it was preached in Corinth, Rome, Galatia, Ephesus, Philippi, Colosse, Thessalonica, and in every other place to which Paul or any other apostle went.

3. After one of the apostles had been a long

time engaged in preaching "The gospel of the kingdom" he wrote to some who had heard it, saying, "Though we, or an angel from heaven preach any OTHER gospel unto you than that which WE have preached unto you, let him be accursed. As we said before, so say I now again, If ANY man preach any OTHER gospel unto you than that ye have received, let him be accursed."—Gal. i, 8, 9.

These three great truths may be expressed in the following short and easily remembered sentence,—The Lord Jesus and His apostles preached THE GOSPEL OF THE KINGDOM; and a double curse has been pronounced against man or angel who shall dare to preach *any other gospel*.

And now, in the face of all these facts, is it not surprising to find some persons taking an isolated text (1 Cor. xv, 3, 4,) and, contrary to sound criticism and right interpretation, endeavoring to prove from it that Paul at Corinth did not preach the kingdom, but preached only the death, burial and resurrection of the Saviour? In that text the words *en prōtois*, translated "first of all," are defined by Liddell & Scott's Lexicon (1849) to be "like the Latin in primis, *among* the first." The phrase might be accurately rendered "among primaries." Campbell's edition (A. D. 1832) says, "among the first things." Whitby's paraphrase says, "among the principal doctrines of faith." Thus we see that the death, burial and resurrection although essential things were not the *only* things preached at Corinth but were comprised "among" certain other things elsewhere called "the things concerning the *kingdom of God.*"—Ac. xix, 8.

Those preachers who declaim against us must admit that it would be a wretched sophism, extremely stupid and unfair, to take Ac. xx, 25, and argue from it that the death, burial and resurrection of Christ were not preached or believed in at Ephesus, merely because those events are not mentioned in that text. Now on the *same* principle it would be an equally stupid and unfair sophism to take 1 Cor. xv, 3, 4, and argue from it that the doctrine of the kingdom was not preached or believed in at Corinth, merely because the kingdom is not mentioned in that text. Our opponents try to justify their silence concerning the kingdom by saying that in sundry places conversions are described where there is not express mention of preaching the kingdom. But we rebut this piece of sophistry by proving that in sundry places we have the history of conversions where there *is* express mention of preaching the *kingdom.*—See Ac. viii, 12 : xix, 8, 20 : xx 25 : xxviii, 23, 31. And now let me emphasize this question—whether is it wiser or safer to *include* "the things of the kingdom" in our preaching and faith; and thus have a *whole* and *true* gospel; or to leave out those things of the kingdom as though they were never mentioned in Scripture, and thus have a fragmentary and perverted gospel? To all men, women and children, of common sense, this question is submitted.

To suppose from such texts as 1 Cor. xv, 3, 4, that Paul at Corinth did not preach the gospel of the kingdom, nor require the Corinthians to believe it, is to misunderstand those texts, and to absurdly set Paul against Paul, for it would be accusing him of preaching a very different faith and hope in Corinth from what he preached in Ephesus and Rome; and indeed from what all the apostles were required to preach everywhere, for the command was general, "This gospel of the kingdom shall be preached in *all* the world."—Mat. xxiv, 14. Since therefore the gospel of the kingdom covers the *whole field* of apostolic preaching, it is plain that whatever short phrase is used to designate what was preached at Corinth and other places, "This gospel of the kingdom" is always *implied* if not expressed in that phrase. In 1 Cor. xv, 3, 4, it is implied in the official title "Christ," which means "Anointed."—Jno. i, 41. He is anointed for the *three* offices of *Prophet*, to teach; *Priest*, to intercede; and *King*, to reign. The "great salvation" is comprised in the performance of these three offices. We are by nature ignorant, guilty and enslaved. To remove ignorance is the office of a prophet; to remove guilt, the office of a priest; and to liberate, lead to victory and protect in a safe home and country is the office of a king. The Redeemer's prophetical office was foretold in Isa. lxi, 1–3;—"The Lord hath *anointed* me to preach good tiding unto the meek," etc. His priestly office in Dan. ix, 26 ;—"After threescore and two weeks shall Messiah (i. e. the *Anointed*) be cut off, but not *for himself;*" which means that He "died for *our* sins." His Kingly office in Psa. ii;—"The rulers take counsel together against the Lord and against His *Anointed* (rendered Christ in Ac. iv, 26) . . . Yet have I set my *King* upon my holy hill of *Zion*. . . . I shall give thee the heathen for thine inheritance, and the *uttermost parts of the earth* for thy possession." Here the *territory* and the *royal city* of the king are specified with the utmost clearness.

And now if it be enquired, "How did Christ perform the office of Prophet?" I answer, by teaching men the will of God, personally when He was on earth and afterwards in giving them the Holy Scriptures. How does He perform the office of Priest? By having once offered himself a Sacrifice on the cross, and by still making intercession as the one Mediator between God and man. How will He perform the office of king? By descending from heaven, liberating the righteous from the bondage of sin and sorrow, giving them the victory over death and blessing them with endless life and happiness in the everlasting kingdom which He will then establish on the earth.

And so we see that the title "Christ" is a very comprehensive one. That it includes the doctrine of the kingdom can also be seen by comparing the 5th and 12th verses of Ac. viii, for while one verse tells us that Philip preached "Christ" the other explains it by saying that he preached "the things concerning the kingdom of God and the name of Jesus Christ." I have now proved that the apostles preached and the early christians believed the gospel of the kingdom. And no man in his senses ought to dispute the self-evident assertion that *we* are required to believe the *same* gospel; for there is but one true gospel, one faith and one hope, for all times, places and people, from the apostolic age until now.—Ephes, iv, 4.-6 Jude. 3.

By instructive illustrations I have shown the importance of comparing Scripture with Scripture. Our Lord has left us an example of this: "Beginning at Moses and all the prophets, he expounded unto them in all the Scriptures the things concerning himself."—Lu. xxiv. 27. And the first chapter of Hebrews contains many quotations, *culled* from a wide field of Scripture, on the subject of the superiority of Christ to angels. For readily finding the testimonies on any subject, a Concordance and a Bible with a good selection of marginal references will be of great service. Although the marginal references were not arranged by inspiration, but are a human work and therefore imperfect in some instances, yet a discriminating reader will still find them serviceable; and indeed it is wonderful what a vast amount of accurate and valuable information can be obtained by their assistance. For example, in studying the first verse of the New Testament, the marginal references are of thrilling interest. From Abraham to David were fourteen, and from David to Christ were twenty-eight generations; we are naturally led to enquire, therefore, Why is the Saviour called the Son of David, the son of Abraham, all the preceding and intervening patriarchs being left out of that verse? In following out the marginal references we discover that it is because two great covenants have been made, the one with Abraham, and the other with David, which covenants are to be fulfilled in Christ the divine "Seed" or Son of whom they speak. Thus on the phrase, "the Son of David," the reference takes us to Ac. ii, 30, where Peter tells us, in his great Pentecostal sermon that God hath sworn with an oath to David "that of the fruit of his loins according to the flesh he would raise up Christ to sit on his throne." Thus, as the son of David, he will inherit David's throne. From Acts ii, 30, the reference takes us to 2 Sam. vii, 12, 13, where we find the covenant with David, containing the oath to which Peter refers. Then to Psa. cxxxii, 11, where the same oath is referred to in almost the exact words of Peter, "The Lord hath sworn in truth unto David, he will not turn from it, of the fruit of thy body will I set upon thy throne." Then to Luke i, 32, 33, where also the angel Gabriel declares that Christ shall obtain the throne of his father David, and that "of his kingdom there shall be no end." And now see how the light accumulates and grows brighter and still brighter, as we progress in our researches! for here the reference is to Dan. ii, 44; vii, 14, 27, where we learn that when Christ obtains the throne of David, his kingdom will not be confined to the narrow strip of land over which David reigned, but will fill the *whole* earth; also that it will be an everlasting kingdom, and will be *under* the whole heaven, and therefore on earth, of course.

Then we are taken to Obadiah 21, and there told that the kingdom shall be the *Lord's,* that is, it will be the kingdom of God, spoken of in the gospel. Thence we are referred to Rev. xi, 15, which informs us that the kingdom will be manifested at the resurrection season, under the seventh trumpet, which is "the *last* trumpet." Then to Rev. xix, 6, etc., where we learn that the Lord Jesus will not obtain the kingdoms of this world without opposition, for the vile kings of the earth and their armies will make war with the Lamb, but the Lamb shall overcome them, and bind Satan, and reign triumphantly with his risen saints in the blissful millennial state.—Rev. xviii, 14; xx.

And now, returning to our verse we take up the other phrase, "the Son of Abraham." The reference here points to Gal. iii, 16, which informs us that to Christ as the "Seed" or Son of Abraham, certain great promises have been made. And the reference there points to Gen. xii, 7, where the promise reads thus, "Unto thy seed will I give *this* land," meaning the land of Canaan on this earth. And the reference here points to Gen. xiii, 15; xvii. 8, where we discover that all the land of Canaan has been promised for an *everlasting* possession, to Abraham and his seed, that is, to Abraham and to Christ, as Paul explains it. Thus the argument is perfectly clear that as the Son of Abraham, the Lord Jesus will inherit the *land* of Canaan on this earth, for an everlasting or eternal possession; and as the son of David, he will inherit a glorious *throne* upon that land.

Now returning to Gal. iii, I find on verse 17 a reference to Rom. iv. 13, which gives us to understand that the full extent of the promise was equal to the promise of "*the world,*" for, as we have shown, when the Son of David (and Son of God) comes in glory and takes possession of the throne of David his kingdom will fill the whole earth. Then in verse 29 of Gal. iii, I find that all Christians, by virtue of their relationship to Christ, are also Abraham's seed, and heirs according to the promise made to him and his seed. And the reference on this verse takes us to Rom. viii, 17, which says that they are *joint heirs* with Christ.

Behold, then, how these two classes of testimony—the one concerning the Son of David, the other concerning the Son of Abraham—are like two crystal streams that, rising in the first verse of the New Testament, flow throughout the Scriptures, gathering volume from their tributary texts as they go, until they both end and blend

> In that bright Paradise restor'd
> The blissful kingdom of the Lord:

Even in that kingdom which the Lord Jesus will establish on earth at His coming, and in which, through the atoning merits of the precious blood of Christ you may obtain endless happiness if you will believe and obey the gospel of the kingdom.

SECOND DISCOURSE.

"WHAT MUST I DO TO BE SAVED?"

"Then he called for a light, and sprang in, and came trembling, and fell down before Paul and Silas, and brought them out, and said, Sirs, what must I do to be saved? And they said, Believe on the Lord Jesus Christ, and thou shalt be saved, and thy house."—ACTS XVI, 29, 30, 31.

This thrilling piece of apostolic history contains the most important question that can be framed by human lips. It is not what must I do to obtain health, or wealth, or fame, or some high position of human power and grandeur; but infinitely more than all these, "What must I do to *be saved?*" And in proportion to the importance of the question is the plainness of the answer, "Believe on the Lord Jesus Christ." Belief and faith are the same; and what this answer requires is, of course, not a faith without works, which is dead; but it requires a living faith—a faith which "works by love and purifies the heart."—Jas. ii, 20.

I have called this a very plain answer, because, with the Bible before us, it is easy to discover what is meant by believing on the Lord Jesus Christ. The subject is placed before us in the clearest light. For example, we know that a message sent makes him by whom it is sent a messenger, and that to truly believe on the messenger is to believe the message which he brings. Now, among his other attributes, we find those of a messenger expressly attributed to Christ, and that he has been sent as the bearer of *a message* from God to man. Thus he is called the "Messenger of the covenant."— Mal. iii, 1. "The Apostle and High Priest of our profession."—Heb. iii, 1. The word "apostle" here applied to the Lord Jesus, conveys the same idea, for it means "a messenger, ambassador." And in the parable of the vineyard the Saviour speaks of himself in the same way—" last of all he *sent unto them his Son.*" Again he says, "I am *sent to preach* the kingdom of God." At the house of Cornelius, Peter also called attention to "the *word which God sent* unto the children of Israel, preaching peace by Jesus Christ."—Acts x, 36. The Father says, "This is my beloved Son, hear him."—Lu. ix, 35. And Moses said, "Him shall ye hear in *all things whatsoever* he shall say unto you. And it shall come to pass that every soul which will not hear that prophet shall be *destroyed*."—Acts iii, 22, 23.

To make the subject still clearer, we find the Lord Jesus placed before us also in the attitude of a *witness* bearing *testimony*. Thus he is called "The Faithful and True Witness."—Rev. iii, 14. And he declares of himself, "For this cause came I into the world, that I should *bear witness* unto the truth."—John xviii, 37. Now the message or doctrine which he preached is "His *testimony*," and the Scriptures assure us that " He that hath received his *testimony* hath set to his seal that God is true"; but on the other hand, " He that *believeth not* the Son shall not see life, but the wrath of God abideth on him."—John iii, 33, 36.
We have now shown, by varied illustration and overwhelming proof, that to "believe on the Lord Jesus Christ," in a true and Scriptural sense, is to believe and obey that message or testimony which he has proclaimed to men.

What then is that message or testimony which is so essential to salvation ? Our eternal destiny depends on a truthful answer to this question ; and the Lord be praised that we are not left in the dark on a subject of such vast importance. Peter has with great precision pointed out the path by which we can find what that message was. He says that "the word which God sent unto the children of Israel, preaching peace by Jesus Christ . . . was published throughout all Judea, and began from

Galilee, after the baptism which John preached." Acts x, 36, 37. With such "great plainness of speech" as this, how is it possible for us to miss that word or message for which we are searching? We are told, 1st, Who sent it—" the word which God sent"; 2nd, To whom it was sent—" unto the children of Israel"; 3rd, By whom it was sent—" by Jesus Christ"; 4th, In what region it was published—" throughout all Judea"; 5th, From what point it began—" from Galilee"; 6th, At what time it began—" after the baptism which John preached." Such plain directions take us directly to Mark i, 14, which says, " Now after that John was put in prison, Jesus came into Galilee, preaching THE GOSPEL OF THE KINGDOM OF GOD." How accurately this answers to the language of Peter! John "was a bright and shining light," but his ministry had now come to a close. His voice had been hushed on the banks of the Jordan. Eager crowds no longer thronged its verdant slopes—all was silence and solitude there; for John had been torn away from his holy work and shut up in a dark and gloomy prison. And there he was put to death as the reward of a cruel young woman for dancing. Contrast her conduct with that of the pious Esther who fasted and prayed to *save* life. Who then can love dancing, after seeing that it caused the murder of one of whom the Saviour said, " Among them that are born of women there hath not risen a greater."

But although the Lord allows his workmen to be buried, he carries on his work; for after John's voice was hushed, the blessed Saviour "began from Galilee" proclaiming "*The gospel of the kingdom of God.*" Another portion of Scripture informs us that he "went about all Galilee, teaching in their synagogues and preaching *the gospel of the kingdom.*"—Matthew iv, 23. Nor did he confine his ministry to that section, but published the same great message "throughout all Judea," as we learn from Luke viii, 1—"It came to pass afterward that he went throughout every city and village, preaching and showing *the glad tidings of the kingdom of God.*" When the people of Capernaum urged him to stay longer with them he refused, saying "I must preach *the kingdom of God* to other cities also; for therefore am I sent."—Luke iv, 43. And even in that solemn interval between his resurrection and ascension his theme was still "the things pertaining to *the kingdom of God.*"—Acts i, 3.

Thus I have plainly and abundantly proved that "THE GOSPEL OF THE KINGDOM" is the great message or testimony which Christ has brought to men. It follows, therefore, that "*The gospel of the kingdom*" is what we must believe before we can be truly said to "believe on the Lord Jesus Christ." He has *commanded* us to believe that gospel. "Jesus came into Galilee preaching the gospel of the kingdom of God, and saying, 'Repent ye, and believe the gospel'."—Mark i, 14, 15. Of course He did not command them to believe "*another* gospel" than the one that He was preaching. The language, therefore, proves that He commanded them to believe the identical gospel that He was preaching—" the gospel of the kingdom of God." Does any one imagine that it is not essential to keep His commandments? "Why call ye me Lord, Lord, and do not the things which I say?"—Lu. vi, 46. " Ye are my friends if ye do whatsoever I command you."—John xv, 14. " *Whatsoever He* saith unto you *do*."—John ii, 5. " If ye *love* me keep my commandments."—John xiv, 15. Keeping His commandments is a *test* of our *loving* Him, and certainly no one can be saved who does *not* love Him, for the fearful penalty has been pronounced, "If any man love not the Lord Jesus Christ let him be Anathema Maranatha," i. e. accursed when the Lord comes.—1 Cor. xvi, 22.

Because the Son of God has set us the example and made the kingdom of God the great and constant theme of his discourse, we know this must be the wisest, noblest and best theme that can occupy the minds or tongues of men. But it is well known that multitudes of modern teachers, both in high and low positions, with a blind and fatal persistency, refuse to either believe or preach that blessed gospel of the kingdom. For all the world I would not be in the place of such teachers at the day of judgment. A prominent member of a popular denomination once told me that he had been attending his church twenty-five years, but did not remember ever having heard that expression—the gospel of the kingdom—used there, or to have heard a sermon preached on it. A preacher of another large and popular sect told me that he remembered the expression, "the gospel of the kingdom," and he believed that it occurred "somewhere in the Epistles." Another preacher who said he had studied Greek and Hebrew, had graduated regularly in theology, and had been preaching six years; on being questioned by me as to whether the expression "the gospel of the kingdom" occurs in the Old or New Testament, said that he believed it occurred in the Old Testament, "perhaps in the Psalms," and that he had never preached a sermon on the subject. But, according to Cruden's Concordance, that expression is not once found in the Epistles, the Psalms, nor in the Old Testament at all. Do not these incidents prove that a great apostasy has taken place in the world, and that men have "departed from the faith" and fallen into the pernicious practice of preaching "another gospel" than that which the Lord Jesus preached? And not only did the Lord himself preach the kingdom of God, but while his own personal ministry was going on "He called his twelve disciples together and .... sent *them* to preach the kingdom of God. And they departed and went through the towns preaching the gospel."—Luke ix, 2, 6. Here we discover, that in Scriptural phraseology, preaching the kingdom is the same as preaching the gospel. It follows, therefore, that those who do not preach the kingdom do not preach the gospel. So important is preaching the kingdom that when a certain man requested leave to first go and bury his father, the Lord said, "Let the dead bury their dead; but go thou and preach the kingdom of God."—Luke ix, 60.

But the gospel of the kingdom was not restricted to Palestine, for towards the close of his personal ministry the Saviour said, "This gospel of the kingdom shall be preached in *all* the world."—Matt. xxiv, 14. This language was both a prophecy and a command. By examining the record we discover that this prophecy was not to be fulfilled, nor this command obeyed, until after Pentecost; it is therefore the only true gospel of the present dispensation. I say the apostles did not go into all the world until *after* Pentecost, because until then the limits of their ministry had kept them in Palestine—"Go not into the way of the Gentiles, and into any city of the Samaritans enter ye not."—Matt. x, 5. This was before the Saviour ascended. And when he was about to ascend he charged them, "Tarry ye in the city of Jerusalem, until ye be endued with power from on high."—Luke xxiv, 49. While preaching in Judea they needed only to know the language of that land; but now that they were to go into all the world, they needed to be endued with power to speak the languages of the various nations to whom they were sent. This power was conferred on them in the gift of tongues on the day of Pentecost, about ten days after the Lord ascended. Thenceforth nothing hindered them from going into all the world and preaching the gospel of the kingdom to every creature, agreeably to the prophecy and command of the Saviour, who had also said, "Ye shall be witnesses unto me both in Jerusalem and in all Judea, and in Samaria, and unto the uttermost parts of the earth."—Acts i, 8. Thus we perceive that the gospel of the kingdom was as *universal* in the apostolic preaching as the baptismal formula was in their baptizing. We rightly conclude that baptizing "into the name of the Father, and of the Son, and of the Holy Spirit," was practiced everywhere by the apostles, although we find that precise formula but once in the Bible; once being quite enough to render it a law.—Matt. xxviii, 19. On the same principal of interpretation we must conclude that "the gospel of the kingdom" was preached everywhere the apostles went, for the words of the Master—"this gospel of the kingdom shall be preached in *all* the world"—most plainly required them to preach it. And this is even clearer, if possible, than the universality of the baptismal formula; for we have frequent allusion to the preaching of the kingdom by the apostles. Thus we find Philip in Samaria "preaching the things concerning the kingdom of God, and the name of Jesus Christ."—Acts viii, 12. Also Paul in Ephesus, and other places, preaching "the things concerning the kingdom of God."—Acts xix, 8; xx, 25. In Rome he dwelt two whole years, "preaching the kingdom of God, and teaching those things which concern the Lord Jesus Christ." —Acts xxviii, 23, 31.

As the Bible teaches but one faith and one hope, so also it recognizes but one *gospel*, and pronounces a double curse on man or angel who shall dare to "preach *any* other gospel."—Eph. iv, 5; Gal. i, 8, 9. And now, after the preceding testimonies, can you doubt what is that one gospel? Surely it can be none other than "*This gospel of the kingdom,*" which the Saviour said should "be preached in all the world;" and which was carried to one place "as" to another, for Paul tells the Colossians that it had to come unto them "as (*kathōs* just as) in all the world."—Col. i, 6, 23. And since there is but one gospel, it follows that it is "*this gospel of the kingdom*" of which the Bible says, "He that believeth not shall be damned."—Mark xvi, 15, 16. Behold then the awful penalty of either preaching or believing "any other gospel" than "this gospel of the kingdom."

Of course, to preach the gospel of the kingdom is not to merely repeat that phrase again and again in the hearing of the people; for what information could they possibly gain by such a procedure? The word translated "gospel" (*euaggelion*) means "a good message, glad tidings, joyful news." To preach the gospel of the kingdom therefore is to preach those things which constitute the good message, or "glad tidings of the kingdom." This is illustrated in the case of Philip who in Samaria preached the gospel of the kingdom by preaching "the things concerning the kingdom of God, and the name of Jesus Christ."—Acts viii, 12. And we know that the preaching of Philip, in Samaria harmonized with that of Paul in Corinth, and with that of all the apostles in all places; for there was but *one* gospel preached by them all. As Moses did not give two or more opposite codes of law for the Mosaic dispensation; so neither did Christ give two or more opposite gospels for the present dispensation. But as anciently there were some who perverted the law of Moses by their tradition, so now there are some who pervert the gospel of the kingdom by their tradition. Since, however, it was necessary for the Samaritans to believe "the things concerning the kingdom of God, and the name of Jesus Christ," it is just as necessary for us to believe the *same* things; for it is our duty to "hold fast the form of sound words;" to "earnestly contend for the faith once delivered to the saints;" to "ask for the old paths and walk in them."—2 Tim. i, 13; Jude 3; Jer. vi, 16.

We have now proved that the only way to preach or believe the gospel of the kingdom is to preach or believe those great truths of which that gospel consists. This brings us to the important question, "Of what truths does that gospel consist?" Those truths, according to the plain teaching of the Bible, are—

1. That it will be a *divine* kingdom, as its name implies—"the kingdom of heaven," or "the kingdom of God." It is called by these names because it is a kingdom which "the God of heaven will set up."—Dan. ii, 44. It will be as far superior to human kingdoms as light is superior to darkness. But although its king and princes will be spiritual beings, yet they will be none the less really present in bodily and tangible form. If this audience were composed of angels instead of mortals, it would be strictly a spiritual audience, and yet visible and tangible, for the angels have tangible and visible bodies. Three dined at the tent door of Abraham, and he brought water to wash their feet. Afterwards, two lodged in the house of Lot, ate unleavened cakes, and grasped him and his family by the hands to hurry them out of Sodom. One wrestled with Jacob, and by a touch caused him to limp; "for a token" as Scott says, "that it was a *reality*, and not a *dream*, or *vision*, or *delusive imagination*." Of course, Jacob could not lay hold on and wrestle with an intangible "*ghost*." Well, we know that the risen and glorified saints

will be "equal unto the angels;" yea more, the blessed Redeemer will "change" (not annihilate) their bodies, and fashion them "like unto *his* glorious body."—Luke xx, 36; Phil. iii, 21. And we have many "infallible proofs" that his body was visible and tangible, for it came forth from the tomb after the stone was rolled away; it had "flesh and bones," and could be seen and handled; he did also eat and drink with his disciples after his resurrection.—Luke xxiv, 39, 40; Acts i, 3; x, 41.

2. The Scriptures also testify that the kingdom, although divine and heavenly or heaven-like, will be *on this earth*. The covenants with Abraham and David show that a gracious *necessity* exists for the return of Christ and His reign in Jerusalem over the land of Canaan and the whole earth. We see not how those "promises made unto the fathers" can ever be fulfilled unless He shall return, take possession of the earth, and establish His kingdom here. When the Lord Jesus says "my kingdom is not of this world," he does not mean that it will not be on the earth, but rather that it is not of this world as to *origin* or *source*; for the preposition *ek* translated "of," is frequently used with reference to the origin or source of a thing. So the apostles and the baptism of John were truly and literally on the earth and in the world; and yet the baptism was not "of (*ek*) men," nor were the apostles "of (*ek*) the world." Certainly those who say that the church is the kingdom admit that the kingdom is

in the world, for the church is here. The territory or land-basis of the kingdom is a prominent item of the gospel of the kingdom. Almost the first thing that a school-boy finds in his geography concerning any human kingdon is a description of its *whereabouts*, its *territory*, its *area*, etc. Then he reads of the royal family, the capital city, the constitution, the condition of the populace, etc. And this illustrates, in some degree, the method in which the Bible treats of that divine kingdom which is the great theme of Scripture, from Genesis to Revelation.

The Saviour said, "The kingdom of heaven is like unto a grain of mustard seed, which a man took, and sowed *in* his *field*." He afterwards explained to his disciples that "the field is *the world*." —Matt. xiii, 31, 38. This teaches most plainly, that the kingdom, though a celestial germ, is to be implanted and to grow in terrestrial soil. And the same is taught "without a parable," when the disciples, though on earth, are told to pray, "Thy kingdom *come*." The New Jerusalem will be on earth, and "the THRONE of God and of the Lamb shall be *in it;*" hence that throne also will be on earth.—Rev. xxi, 2, 10, with xxii, 3. Could we desire any plainer language than the assurance that "his dominion shall be from sea even to sea, and from the river to the ends of the earth."—Zech. ix, 10. That it shall fill "the *whole* earth."—Dan. ii, 35. That "the kingdom, the dominion and the greatness of the kingdom *under* the whole heaven shall be given to the people of the saints of the Most High?"—Dan. vii, 27. That "the kingdoms of this world" shall become our Lord's and his Christ's?—Rev. xi, 15. That Christ shall have the heathen for his inheritance and "the uttermost parts of *the earth*" for his possession?—Psalm ii, 8. Surely I have quoted testimony enough to prove, beyond the shadow of a doubt, that the kingdom will be on earth. The celebrated Dean Alford says, "That the Lord will come *in person* to this our earth; that His *risen elect* will reign *here* with Him and judge; that during that blessed reign the power of evil will be bound, and the glorious prophecies of peace and truth on earth find their accomplishment;—this is my firm persuasion, and not mine alone, but that of multitudes of Christ's waiting people, *as it was of his primitive apostolic church.*"—Prol. to vol. iv of N. T.

3. That it will be an *everlasting* kingdom, that shall not pass away, and of which there shall be no end. In proof of this I need only refer you to the following testimonies: "Of his kingdom there shall be no end."—Luke i, 33. "The everlasting kingdom of our Lord and Saviour Jesus Christ."—2 Pet. i, 11. "His dominion is an everlasting dominion, which shall not pass away, and his kingdom that which shall not be destroyed."—Dan. vii, 14, 27. "The God of heaven shall set up a kingdom which shall never be destroyed; and the

kingdom shall not be left to other people, but it shall break in pieces and consume all these kingdoms, and it shall stand forever."—Dan. ii, 44.

4. That Jesus is the Christ, the Son of God, and has been appointed by the Father to be the King in that kingdom. Nathaniel confessed, "Rabbi, thou art the Son of God, thou art the King of Israel."—John i, 49. Peter also confessed, Thou art the Christ, the son of the living God." —Mat. xvi, 16. It is to Him that the Father says, "I will give thee the heathen for thine inheritance, and the uttermost parts of the earth for thy possession."—Psa. ii, 8. It is of him the prophet says, "His dominion shall be from sea even to sea, and from the river to the ends of the earth." —Zech. ix, 10. He is called the "mighty God," and will come in the *glory of his Father* to take his seat on the throne.—Isa. ix, 6, 7; Mat. xxv, 31. Accordingly the kingdom is called "the kingdom of Christ *and* of God."—Eph. v, 5; "the kingdom of our Lord *and* his Christ."—Rev. xi, 15; "the everlasting kingdom of our Lord and Saviour Jesus Christ."—2 Pet. i, 11. Peter, in saying that an entrance *shall be*—not has been— ministered to the saints into that kingdom, shows that the kingdom is yet *future;* while Daniel (vii, 27) in saying of the very same kingdom that it shall be "*under* the whole heaven," shows that it will be on *earth*. Now by adding together these two testimonies, we discover that God is *hereafter*

to establish an everlasting kingdom on earth, into which all who hold out faithful are *yet to enter.* This argument alone proves that the kingdom is not the church, but the *reward* of the church. To his church the Lord has promised, saying " Fear not little flock, for it is your Father's good pleasure to give to you the kingdom."—Luke xii, 32. And when will he give it to the little flock? Mark well the answer:—" When the Son of man shall come in his glory, and all the holy angels with him, then shall he sit upon the throne of his glory. . . . *Then* shall the King say unto them on his right hand, Come, ye blessed of my Father, inherit the kingdom."—Mat. xxv, 31, 34.

5. That in order to obtain an inheritance in that kingdom a person must become *righteous* ; " for the unrighteous shall not inherit the kingdom of God."—1 Cor. vi, 9. It is " promised to them that *love* him," Jas. ii, 5 ; to " the *saints* of the Most High," Dan. vii, 18, 22 ; to the " little flock," Luke xii, 32 ; to "the righteous," Mat. xxv, 34, 37. Therefore the Saviour directs us to "seek first the kingdom of God and his *righteousness.*"—Mat. vi, 33. The kingdom is the aim and end ; righteousness is the road to it. That righteousness comes only through Christ, and by the merits of his atonement, or *at-one-ment,* as the word implies. " Christ died for our sins."—1 Cor. xv, 3. " By the obedience of one shall many be made righteous."—Rom. v, 19. " Christ is the end of the

law for righteousnesss to every one that believeth." Rom. x, 4.

That righteousness, long ago purchased by the precious blood of Christ, is now individually applied to the believer of the gospel of the kingdom when he is baptized *for the remission of sins;* for such is the plain requirements of Scripture, " repent and be baptized every one of you, in the name of Jesus Christ, for the remission of sins"—"arise and be baptized and *wash away thy sins,* calling on the name of the Lord."—Acts ii, 38; xxii, 16. After the believer has been thus baptized, he is said to be in Christ; and if any man be in Christ Jesus, he is a new creature, for there is no condemnation to them that are in Christ Jesus, who walk not after the flesh but after the Spirit.—2 Cor. v, 17; Rom. viii, 1.

6. And that in order to inherit the kingdom a person must also be made *immortal;* for flesh and blood cannot inherit the kingdom of God.—1 Cor. xv, 50. On this text Adam Clarke has truly said: " Man in his present state cannot inherit the kingdom of God; his nature is not suited to that place. . . . Paul is certainly not speaking of flesh and blood in a moral sense, to signify corruption of mind and heart; but in a natural sense." Scott also, after describing the change which takes place in those who shall arise from the grave, says, " A similar change must also be made in the bodies of those who shall be found alive at the day of judg-

ment: for flesh and blood, the human body in its present form and gross manner of subsistence, and with its present animal wants, propensities, and infirmities, cannot inherit the kingdom of God."

That immortality is to be obtained through Christ alone, at the resurrection. "The wages of sin is death, but the gift of God is eternal life through our Lord Jesus Christ."—Rom. vi, 23. "This corruptible must put on incorruption, and this mortal must put on immortality. So, when this corruptible shall have put on incorruption, and this mortal shall have put on immortality, then shall be brought to pass the saying that is written, death is swallowed up in victory. O death, where is thy sting? O grave, where is thy victory?—1 Cor. xv, 53-55.

I have now proved that TO BELIEVE ON THE LORD JESUS CHRIST IS TO BELIEVE THE GOSPEL OF THE KINGDOM, WHICH TEACHES THAT HE WILL COME AND ESTABLISH THAT KINGDOM ON EARTH, AND GIVE TO THE RIGHTEOUS ENDLESS LIFE AND HAPPINESS THEREIN, AT THE RESURRECTION.

This is that "great salvation which at the first began to be spoken by the Lord, and was confirmed unto us by them that heard him."—Heb. ii, 3. "*How* shall we escape if we *neglect* so great salvation?" This is a solemn question which neither man nor angel can answer, for there is no escape for any who neglect it. You need not revile or oppose, but merely *neglect it,* to insure your destruction. You have heard the question, "What must I do to be saved?" Now if you ask "What must I do to be *lost?*" I answer, "Do *nothing!* you are rushing along the track to perdition; just keep your seat, you need not change cars at all; remain as you are, without hope, without Christ, and without God in the world; go away from here to-day just as you came; continue to neglect—only to neglect—so great salvation; and you cannot escape the consuming wrath of God." Do you protest that you have not committed any great sin to deserve such a fate? I answer, that the sin of omission—the sin of *not* believing—is a great sin and worthy of death; for "he that believeth not shall be damned."—Mark xvi, 16. "Without faith it is impossible to please God."—Heb. xi, 6. So you see, that if your entire life until now could have been pure as the white lily in the morning dew, this would not relieve you from the necessity of believing the gospel of the kingdom.

I have shown you that the Son of God preached the gospel of the kingdom, and that "he that believeth not the Son shall not see life; but the wrath of God abideth on him."—John iii, 36. Oh, think of the wrath of God! The wrath of him of whose power and sublimity we have astonishing examples in the creation of man—of the starry sky—of the troubled ocean—of majestic rivers—deafening cataracts—lofty mountains—volcanoes—earthquakes the solar system—the universe. Of him in whose path yonder great blazing sun is but as a glittering sand; while the myriads of stars that form the Milky-way are as trembling white lilies that fringe the pearly track of his chariot wheels. Of the wrath of him with whom "the nations are as a drop of a bucket, and are counted as the small dust of the balance."—Isa. xl, 15. "O, who can stand before his indignation, and who can abide the fierceness of his anger?"—Nahum i, 6

Unless you believe, you will have to "*die in your sins.*" O how different is this from dying in Christ—from falling asleep in Jesus—from dying the death of the righteous and having your last end like his! Have you never thought of the kind of death you would prefer? When quite a young man I attended on several occasions at the bedside of a gentleman who was dying of dropsy; and the excruciating pain he suffered as the water rose higher and higher, and crowded around his heart, filled my mind with a horror of that disease, and caused me to inwardly pray that the Lord would never allow me to die that way. But what is that compared to the pain and horror of dying *in your sins?*

Better die in the deepest and most fearful dungeon that the ingenuity and cruelty of man could invent, than to die in your sins. Better die in the pest-house, reeking with small pox and every other contagious disease, and avoided by your nearest friends, than to die in your sins. Better die in the devouring jaws of wild beasts, all mangled and torn to pieces, than to die in your sins. Better die in the flames of martyrdom, at the burning stake, surrounded by a hissing crowd of persecutors, than to die in your sins. Better die in a midnight storm, "far, far at sea," and sink down into its dark depths with no eye to pity and no arm to save, your cries of distress being drowned by the roar of the winds and billows, than to die in your sins. Better die in the appalling flash of a thunderbolt, without one moment's warning to say, "God be merciful to me," and with no time to bid farewell to father or mother, sister or brother, wife or children, than to die in your sins. Better die in the fearful spasms of hydrophobia, when it would be considered an act of mercy to smother you between two feather beds, than to die in your sins. Better die on a pallet of straw, in starvation, solitude and neglect, with no one to give you a cup of cold water or a crust of bread, than to die in your sins. And yet surely, surely, you *will* die in your sins unless you believe and obey the gospel of the kingdom.

To speak of *obeying* the gospel implies that it carries with it *commands to be obeyed*, as well as *truths to be believed*. In the great commission under which the apostles were sent into all the world, they were instructed to baptize those who believed. Go, teach all nations, *baptizing* them —" he that believeth and is baptized shall be saved."—Mat. xxxviii, 19; Mark xvi, 15, 16.

And thus it is that in the very first sermon preached by the apostles under that commission, we find them *commanding* their hearers to be "baptized for the remission of sins."—Acts ii, 38. Also when Peter preached at the house of Cornelius the believers were *commanded* to be baptized. Ac. x, 48. In like manner the command was given to Paul "Arise and be baptized and *wash away thy sins.*"—Acts xxii, 16. I might refer to more instances, but these are enough to prove that baptism is one of the great commands of the gospel. And "what shall the end be of them that obey not the gospel?" This question is asked by Peter, and answered by Paul: "The Lord Jesus shall be revealed from heaven in flaming fire taking *vengeance* on them that know not God and obey not the gospel."—1 Pet. iv, 17; 2 Thess. i, 8. But it is a precious privilege that though your sins would hurl you headlong into the consuming billows of the lake of fire, yet you are permitted to go down into the cool and pleasant baptismal waters and wash away thy sins *through the merits of the blood of the Lamb.*

Yes, baptism is a command of God. Then why not be "baptized straightway?" Can you frame an excuse that will be sufficient in the sight of him who knows every thought of your heart? Look at Calvary, and see the tender form of the loving

Saviour stretched upon the cruel cross, and bleeding from his head, his hands, his feet, and even from his heart—*for you!* Surely "the love of Christ constraineth us" to keep His commandments.—2 Cor. v, 14. Look forward to the resurrection morn, and see the pearly gates of the New Jerusalem; over them in blazing letters that gleam far out over hill and vale, behold the words, "Blessed are they that *do* his commandments that they may have right to the tree of life, and may enter in through the gates into the city." See the white-robed and shining ranks of the redeemed; every face is like an angel's face, and beams with unutterable joy, as with eager steps they press through those white and pearly gates that stand wide open to receive them; while from within bright angel-choirs hymn sweet welcomes, and strike their golden harps afresh to sing the triumphs of redeeming love. But who are those who stand in outer darkness, clothed in rags; their eyes all red and swollen with weeping; their faces pinched and shrunken with hunger, thirst and woe? They, too, thought to enter these beautiful gates; but, no, the angels closed the great golden bolts, and pointed to the blazing words above—"Blessed are they that do his commandments, that they may have right to the tree of life, and may enter in through the gates into the city."—Rev. xxii, 14.

O then "why tarriest thou? Arise and be baptized, and wash away thy sins, calling on the name of the Lord." Hear the blessed Saviour's tender and loving invitation—"Come unto me all ye that labor and are heavy laden and I will give you rest; take my yoke upon you and learn of me, for my yoke is easy and my burden is light."—Mat. xi, 28, 30. The Father himself invites you; yes, the great Jehovah himself condescends to plead with you—"Come now, and let us reason together, saith the Lord; though your sins be as scarlet, they shall be white as snow; though they be red like crimson, they shall be as wool."—Isa. i, 18. Angels rejoice over one sinner that repenteth. Saints on earth are glad to welcome you into the Church of Christ. Begin *to-day* to lead the Christian life. The Bible nowhere tells you to put it off until to-morrow, but "to-day if ye will hear his voice, harden not your hearts."

THIRD DISCOURSE.

THE PROMISES MADE UNTO THE FATHERS; OR, THE COVENANT WITH ABRAHAM.

"Now I say that Jesus Christ was a minister of the circumcision for the truth of God, to confirm the promises made unto the fathers."—Rom. xv, 8.

Surely there can be no rational doubt as to the importance of our knowing the blessed Redeemer to whatever extent He has clearly revealed himself in Scripture. Such a knowledge of Him is a mark of our being members of His flock, for He says, "I know my sheep and *am known* of mine." —Jno. x, 14. Hence we are commanded to "Grow in grace and in the knowledge of our Lord Jesus Christ."—2 Pet. iii, 18. Now a clear understanding of this text will greatly increase our knowledge of Him and of that gospel of the kingdom which He and His apostles preached. To obtain a clear understanding of Paul's language in this verse, let us first enquire, *who* are "the fathers?" and then, *what* are "the promises" made to them?

1st. Who are the fathers? Moses was commanded to say to the children of Israel, "The Lord God of your *fathers*, the God of *Abraham*, the God of *Isaac*, and the God of *Jacob* hath sent me unto you."—Ex. iii, 15. And Peter says, "The God of *Abraham*, and of *Isaac*, and of *Jacob*, the God of our *fathers*, hath glorified His Son Jesus."—Ac. iii, 13. These testimonies, one from each Testament, are enough to show that Abraham, Isaac, and Jacob are the fathers. But in another place Paul has clearly enough explained himself and settled the question, saying "To *Abraham* and his seed were THE PROMISES made."—Gal. iii, 16. And because those promises were substantially repeated to Isaac and Jacob they are called "the promises made unto the fathers," in the plural number.

2nd. What are the promises made to them?

They are found in the history of those patriarchs as recorded in Genesis. When Abraham left Mesopotamia and came into the land of Canaan the Lord said to him, "Unto thy seed will I give THIS land. ... Lift up now thine eyes, and look from the place where thou are northward and southward, and eastward, and westward: for all the land which thou seest, to thee will I give it and to thy seed FOREVER. ... The Lord made a COVENANT with Abraham, saying, unto thy seed have I given* THIS land from the river of Egypt unto the great river, the river Euphrates. ... I will establish my COVENANT between me and thee, and thy seed after thee in their generations, for an *everlasting* covenant, to be a God unto thee and to thy seed after thee. I will give unto thee, and to thy seed after thee, the land wherein thou art a stranger, all the land of Canaan for an *everlasting* possession; and I will be their God. ... Thy seed shall possess the gate of his enemies, and in thy seed shall all the nations of the earth be blessed."—Gen. xii, 7: xiii, 14, 15: xv, 18: xvii, 7, 8: xxii, 17, 18.

That substantially the same promises were repeated to Isaac and Jacob is verified by the fact that, about 67 years after the last promise that I

---

* Said " when as yet he had no child, " but " calling those things which be not as though they were," to emphasize the promise.—Ac. vii, 5: Rom. iv, 17.

have quoted, the Lord said to Isaac who was dwelling in the same land, "Unto thee, and unto thy seed, I will give all these countries, and I will perform the oath which I sware unto Abraham thy father. . . And in thy seed shall all the nations of the earth be blessed."–Gen. xxvi, 3, 4. About forty-four years after these promises to Isaac, the Lord said to Jacob, who was also dwelling in the same land, "I am the Lord God of Abraham thy father, and the God of Isaac: the land whereon thou liest, to thee will I give it, and to thy seed. . . . And in thy seed shall all the families of the earth be blessed."—Gen. xxviii, 13, 14. When about to die Jacob said, "God Almighty appeared unto me at Luz in the land of Canaan, and blessed me, and said unto me, Behold I will make thee fruitful and multiply thee, and I will make of thee a multitude of people; and I will give this land to thy seed after thee for an *everlasting* possesssion."—Gen. xlviii, 3, 4.

Having now learned WHAT are the promises, let us bring out their full MEANING by carefully considering the following important points—who are the heirs? where is the inheritance? how long will they hold it? the certainty of the promises; and how may individuals obtain a personal interest in them?

1. Who are the heirs? It is plain enough who Abraham, Isaac and Jacob were, but perhaps there are some who imagine that the word "Seed" here

refers to the Jews who came into the land of Canaan under Joshua. This question, however, is not left to human conjecture, for the inspired Paul has settled it plainly and forever. O that all the world, wherever the Bible is read, would hear this explanation, and would understand its full import.—" To Abraham and his Seed were the promises made. He saith not 'And to seeds,' as of many, but as of ONE, 'And to thy Seed,' WHICH IS CHRIST."— Gal. iii, 16. In these words, "And to thy seed," *kai tō spermati sou,* Paul makes an *exact* quotation, word for word, from the Greek version of Gen. xiii, 15; xvii, 8, both of which places refer to the promise of the *land.* In Gen. xvii, 7, the Greek words are *sou, kai tou spermatos sou,* which literally rendered would be "*of* thee, and *of* thy seed." Neither can Paul's quotation be found in Gen. xxii, 18, for the words there are "and *in* thy seed," *kai en tō spermati sou.* Common fairness requires us to observe the critical *exactness* of the quotation, which is a key to its meaning. That Paul refers to the *land* is further evident from his calling it "the inheritance," ver. 18. Because the promise of the landed inheritance is so often *repeated,* and involves or comprehends within itself so many other promises, it may rightly be called "the promises," in the plural.

---

* Lightfoot, a celebrated Greek and Hebrew scholar, viewed the words, "And to thy seed" as quoted from Gen.

The word "Seed" is frequently used of a single person; it has this meaning in Gen. iii, 15: 2 Saml. vii, 12, as its pronoun "*His*," in the singular number sufficiently proves. And Liddell and Scott's Lexicon refers to various Greek authors who also use it in this way.

Here then we discover that, in the very plainest and most positive manner, a real and tangible inheritance on THIS EARTH has been promised to Abraham, Isaac, Jacob and Christ, for an EVERLASTING or ETERNAL possession. (That everlasting and eternal have the same force, neither more nor less, you may perceive by noticing that "EVERLASTING life" and "ETERNAL life" are used interchangeably and synonymously in the Bible.— Lu. xviii, 30, with Mark x, 30. They are both translations of the *same* Greek word, *aiōnios*.) But the Bible just as clearly shows that although Christ and all of those "fathers" have sojourned personally on that land, yet none of them obtained the promised possession of it. Concerning Abraham it is testified that the Lord " gave him NONE inheritance in it, no, not so much as to set his foot on ; yet He PROMISED that He would give it to him."—Ac. vii, 5. Nor did Isaac and Jacob fare any better, for "all these died in the faith, NOT having received the promises."—Heb. xi, 13, 39.

xiii, 15, and xvii, 8, and he said, " It is true that in both alike the inheritance spoken of refers primarily to the possesion of the land of Canaan."

And the blessed Saviour, in the very zenith of His personal ministry on earth, testified concerning himself that "the foxes have holes and the birds of the air have nests, but the Son of man hath not where to lay His head."—Matt. viii, 20. "He came unto His own (*ta idia*), and His own (*hoi idioi*) received Him not;" or "He came to His own land, and His own people received Him not."—Campbell's edition, 1832.—Jno. i, 11. In Greek the former "His own" is of a different gender from the latter, implying a difference in the meaning.* That land is particularly called Immanuel's by virtue of "the promises."—Isa. viii, 8. But although His enemies rejected and crucified Him, he arose from the dead and ascended to heaven. And from that day until now "the land of promise" has been desecrated by wicked men. But it would be acting the part of an unbeliever to conclude from this that the promises have become a failure, or that they ought to be tortured into some other than their true meaning. "The Scripture cannot be broken."—Jno. x, 35. "Though the vision tarry, wait for it; because it will *surely come*."—Hab. ii, 3.

The blessed Immanuel foresaw that the people then occupying His land would reject Him, and so

---

* "Abundance of passages bear out the meaning which makes *ta idia* His own inheritance or possession i. e. Judea; and *hoi idioi*, the Jews. Compare especially Mat. xxi, 33, &c."—DEAN ALFORD.

He spoke two parables which, viewed in succession, afford a thrilling outline of events from His first coming as a "Lamb" to suffer and die, till His return as a "Lion" to conquer and reign. In the parable of the Vineyard He is "the Heir" of whom the wicked husbandmen say, "Come, let us kill Him, and let us seize on His inheritance."—Mat. xxi, 33-39. This represents His inheritance as on earth, for, of course, they could not expect to seize an inheritance above the skies by killing Him. And having crucified Him, His *resurrection* intervenes at this point, as the golden link which connects this parable with that of the Pounds; for without His resurrection the latter parable could not be fulfilled.—Lu. xix, 12-27. In this parable we behold the risen "*Heir*" as the "*Nobleman,*" arrayed in the princely attire of immortality and going into the "far country to receive for himself a kingdom, and *to return.*" Yes, by a glorious retinue of holy angels, He is escorted from the top of Olivet through the shining pathway of the skies, through the crystal ports of light, and seated at the Father's right hand. And while the bereaved and sorrowing disciples were looking "steadfastly toward heaven as He went up, behold two men stood by them in white apparel; which also said, Ye men of Galilee, why stand ye gazing up into heaven? this *same* Jesus, which is taken up from you into heaven, shall *so come* in like manner as ye have seen Him go into heaven."—Ac. i. 11. The parable of the Pounds is based on the fact that the kings of Judea in those days used, before commencing their reign, to go on a journey to Rome in a far country to be invested with the royalty; after which they would return and reign *in Judea.* Herod and Archelaus are notable instances of this. And so although the Saviour's kingdom will be on earth, He has gone to heaven to receive it, or rather "to procure for himself the *royalty;*" as Campbell's edition, 1832, renders it. He would not accept His crown either from the multitude or from Satan, but only from His omnipotent Father who alone has the right to give it—Jno. vi, 15: Lu. iv, 6, 7.

And when He returns, having been divinely invested with the royalty "*then* shall He sit upon the throne of His glory," and establish in the land of promise a glorious and divine kingdom which will quickly and miraculously "break in pieces" all human kingdoms, and, like a great mountain, fill "the *whole* earth;" for His dominion shall be from sea even to sea, and from the river to the *ends of the earth.*"—Mat. xxv, 31; Dan. ii, 35, 44, Zec. ix, 10. Thus throughout the world He will "possess the gate of His enemies," and great voices will be heard saying, "The kingdoms of this world are become our Lord's and His Christ's; and He shall reign forever and ever."—Gen. xxii, 17; Rev. xi, 15. And because the *full* scope of the promise to Abraham and his seed involves all this *extensive* inheritance, Paul speaks of it as the promise of "*the world.*"—Rom. iv, 13.

But will the merciful Redeemer refuse to associate with himself in that glorious kingdom any of Adam's race except Abraham, Isaac and Jacob; filling all its remaining seats with holy angels from heaven? No, the mercy of God has "provided some better thing" for the sons and daughters of our fallen race. The relationship which every believer sustains to Christ makes that believer a joint heir with Christ. "As many of you as have been baptized into Christ have put on Christ . . . Ye are all one in Christ Jesus. And if ye be Christ's, then are ye Abraham's seed, and heirs according to the promise . . . Heirs of God and JOINT-HEIRS with Jesus Christ."—Gal. iii, 27, 29; Rom. viii, 17. Christ is pre-eminently Abraham's Seed, but believers being reckoned by adoption as all *one* in and *with* Christ, they too are Abraham's seed (though multitudinous) and therefore they are joint-heirs with Him.* So intimate is the union between Christ and believers that they are called "the body of Christ," and "are members of His body, of His flesh, and of His bones."—1 Cor. xii, 27; Ephes. v, 30. They are also, collectively

---

* "This one seed that receives the promise is Christ, and in Him all believers, who constitute His body. All that are united to Christ by faith are in and through Him, Abraham's seed, and heirs of the promise made to Abraham."—Notes of American Tract Society.

and by a figure of speech, called "The Bride the Lamb's wife," all of which proves their joint-heirship with Him.—Rev. xxi, 9. I have now shown that *Christ and the Saints* are the heirs; and that the inheritance will be obtained at the second coming of Christ.

Here let me answer several objections concerning the heirs. I have met some persons who without properly examining the subject have imagined that the promised inheritance was obtained when Israel settled in Canaan under the law of Moses. But this error is at once refuted by the positive declaration of Scripture that *they* "possessed it but A LITTLE WHILE;" whereas the covenant with Abraham promises an *everlasting* possession of it.—Isa. lxiii, 18, with Gen. xvii, 8. And even during the little while of their dwelling upon it, they occupied but a small portion of the large territory covenanted to Abraham; and were forbidden to take the part occupied by the Edomites, Moabites and Ammonites.—Deut. ii, 5, 9, 19. The law or "constitution" under which they were settled positively declared them to be "*sojourners*" i. e. *temporary* residents on the land. Lev. xxv, 23. Hence, in the very height of their national triumph and prosperity, their inspired king David said "We are strangers before thee, and sojourners, as were ALL OF OUR FATHERS."— 1 Chron. xxix, 15; Heb. xi, 9. Their occupation of the land under the law was made *condi-*

tional on their keeping the law.—(Deut. xi, 22, 24); but the covenant with Abraham which after being confirmed was not to be added to, imposed no such conditions as this. Hence the Scripture positively teaches that the inheritance promised to Abraham was not of the law.—Gal. iii, 15, 18. About seven centuries after they entered Canaan a holy prophet spoke of the Abrahamic covenant as still unfulfilled, for he says (not " thou *hast* performed," but) " Thou *wilt* perform the truth to Jacob and the mercy to Abraham which thou hast sworn unto our fathers from the days of old."— Mic. vii, 20. And Paul, glancing at a long succession of good men who lived there during the law, says, " These *all*, having obtained a good report through faith, *received not* the promise: God having provided some better thing for us, that they without us should not be made perfect." Heb. xi, 39, 40.* This reminds us of some great estate of which the older heirs cannot obtain their portion till the younger become of age—till the number of their brethren be made up.—Rev. vi, 11.

In the writings of one Professor Bush, of America, and a Bishop Waldegrave, of England, it has been gravely suggested (apparently with the view of restricting it to Israel under the law) that

---

* " They received not the promises, i. e., the final completion of salvation promised at Christ's coming again: the eternal inheritance, Heb. ix, 15, 28."—The Portable Commentary.

the promise ought to be read "To thee *even* to thy seed" instead of "To thee *and* to thy seed." This would exclude Abraham *personally* from the inheritance. But the common version correctly includes Abraham—"To thee *and* to thy seed." "He promised that He would give it to *him* for a possession *and* to his seed."—Ac. vii, 5. "To Abraham *and* his seed were the promises made." Gal. iii, 16. "To thee *and* to thy seed WITH thee," which implies that the patriarchs and the seed, "which is *Christ*," will both possess it at the *same* time; hence they will then be "ever with the Lord."—Gen. xxviii, 4; 1 Thes. iv, 16, 17. Any rendering which would exclude Abraham *personally* would contradict the word of the Lord who says, "I am the Lord that brought thee out of Ur of the Chaldees, to give *thee* this land to inherit it."—Gen. xv, 7. "I have also established my covenant with them (Abraham, Isaac and Jacob) to give *them* the land of Canaan."—Ex. vi, 4.* Abraham went into the "place which *he*

---

* This text with Ex. iii, 6, shows they will be resurrected and put in possession of the land, for the Saviour quotes the latter text as *proof* of their resurrection.—Lu. xx, 37. The last of these patriarchs had been dead nearly 200 years and yet the inheritance is spoken of (vi, 4) as *yet to be* given; which proves they did not obtain the promised Canaan *at death,* as some imagine. The following is said to occur in the Jewish Talmud.—" In what place does the Law support the resurrection of the dead? Truly when it is said, And I have also established my covenant with them., to give

he should after receive for an inheritance," and dwelt with Isaac and Jacob "the heirs with *him* of the same promise."—Heb. xi, 8, 9. Let us kindly suppose that Bush and Waldegrave were betrayed into making that stupid suggestion through ignorance of the lucid explanation which Paul has given of the promises. If the promised inheritance was only intended for "Israel after the flesh"—the merely natural seed who lived in Canaan under the law of Moses—then not Abraham alone but we also would be excluded from the inheritance. But Paul's inspired explanation most positively forbids the application of the promise to the merely natural Jews under the Mosaic law, for he says that the "seed" specified in the covenant is CHRIST: and hence Abraham and other believers (even allowing the promise to be read, "To thee *even* to thy seed") are not yet disinherited, but rather have their portion *secured* to them in Christ, with whom *all* the righteous are "*joint-heirs.*"—Romans viii, 17. And O! I rejoice that all depends on Christ at last; that He, in whom "all the promises of God" are yea and

---

them the land of Canaan. For it is not said, to give *you*, but to give *them*." Irenæus, pronounced "one of the best Christian writers of the *second* century," speaks of the inheritance promised Abraham, and says, "He shall receive it at the resurrection of the just."—Against Heresies, B. V. ch. xxxii, Edition of Clark, Edinburgh.

amen, is the rich Depositary of all these blessings. 2 Cor. i, 20. In Him our title stands secure, and in Him we read our title clear; not to "mansions in the skies" but in the promised land of Canaan and the whole earth, which, by His beautiful and glorious *presence* will be gladdened and regenerated into an "heavenly country."

2. Where is the inheritance? The promises plainly enough prove that it will be ON EARTH. The demonstrative pronoun "this," five times used, ought to settle that matter. "Unto thy seed will I give THIS land."—"To give thee THIS land."—"THIS land, from the river of Egypt unto the great river, the river Euphrates." Did any one ever hear of such rivers above the skies?—"The Lord God of heaven that sware unto me, saying, Unto thy seed will I give THIS land."—"I will give THIS land to thy seed after thee for an *everlasting* possession."—Gen. xii, 7; xv, 7, 18: xxiv, 7: xlviii, 3, 4. It must be admitted that the holy and inspired Stephen interpreted the promise as referring to a Canaan on earth, for he spoke of it to the wicked Jews as "THIS land wherein *ye* now dwell."—Ac. vii, 4. It was described to Jacob as "The land WHEREON THOU LIEST;" and to Abraham as "The land wherein thou art a stranger."—Gen. xxviii, 13: xvii, 8. And in Heb. xi, 9, we are taught that Abraham actually went "*into* the place (*eis ton topon*) which he should after re-

ceive for an inheritance" and sojourned in it.*
We can form some further idea of the importance
and excellence of that land from the following expressions applied to it in Scripture :—It is called
the Lord's land; Lev. xxv, 23. Immanuel's
land; Isa. viii, 8. The pleasant land; Psa. cvi,
24. The glorious land; Dan. xi, 16, 41. The
glory of all lands; Eze. xx, 6, 15. A *good* land
and *large*, a land flowing with milk and honey; Ex.
iii, 8. A land which the Lord thy God careth for;
the eyes of the Lord thy God are always upon it;
Deut. xi, 12. The holy land; Zec. ii, 12. The
The land of *the promise* (*tēs epaggelias*); Heb. xi,
9. By its central situation it is admirably adapted
to be the royal seat of a world-wide kingdom, being, as it were, the bridge and ligament of three
continents. It extends from the Euphrates on the
East to the river of Egypt and the Mediterranean
Sea on the West; an area of about 300,000 square
miles.—Gen. xv, 18. I have counted thirteen
states of the American Union whose aggregate area
do not amount to this. But, as already shown, the
promise of that land involves the promise of all

---

* Justin Martyr, born about A.D. 114, says, "There shall be a future possession of all the saints in this same land. And hence all men everywhere, whether bond or free, who believe in Christ, and recognize the truth in His own words and those of his prophets, know that they shall be with Him in that land, and inherit incorruptible and everlasting good."—In Dialogue with Trypho, ch. cxxxix, Edition of Clark, Edinburgh, 1870.

lands, for the triumphant kingdom which Christ will establish there shall extend " to the *ends of the earth.*"—Zec. ix, 10. Hence the Father promises to give the *Son* the uttermost parts of the earth for His possession; and the Son promises to make the righteous heirs with himself, saying, " Blessed are the meek for *they* shall inherit the earth."—Psa. ii, 8. Mat. v, 5.

3. How long will they hold it? " Forever." —Gen. xiii, 15.* " For an *everlasting* possession." It will be their " *eternal* inheritance."—Gen. xvii, 8: Heb. ix, 15. If the future *life* will be endless, the future *possession* of the land must also be, for it is the same word, " everlasting," that describes them both. Even in the present existence a man can legally hold his estate so long as his *life* endures; and that the future life of the righteous will be of endless duration is proved not merely by such words as forever, everlasting and eternal, but such expressions as, " they CANNOT DIE any more;" they shall " not perish;" " this mortal shall put on IMMORTALITY, and this corruptible shall put on

---

* " They are not to be heard, which feign that the old Fathers did look only for transitory promises."—Episcopal Creed, Art. vii.

" When we consider that the promises to Abraham have their full completion *in Christ*, to whom are given the uttermost parts of *the earth* for a possession, there need be no *limit* to the sense of the words *for ever.*"—Commentary by Bishops and other Clergy of the church of England.

incorruptibility."—Lu. xx, 36: Jno. iii, 16: 1 Cor. xv, 53. In the very nature of things the promise of everlasting possession *implies* the promise of everlasting LIFE, because as soon as a man dies he ceases to possess his property. And this is the reason why the law could not give that *inheritance* —because it could not give that LIFE which is its indispensable adjunct or correlative. And it could not give that life because it could not give RIGHTEOUSNESS which is the condition that qualifies one for everlasting life.—So Paul argues in Gal. iii, 18, 21. Here there is a most important problem to be solved. We are all sinners by nature and therefore under the direct tendency to that *death* which is "the wages of sin."—Rom. vi, 23. By what means then can we obtain that RIGHTEOUSNESS without which we must come short of the everlasting life and the everlasting inheritance also? Can the law of Moses give us that righteousness? No, "for if righteousness come by the law then Christ died (*apethanen*, past tense,) *in vain*."—Gal. ii, 21. Ah! now the light breaks through the gloom; now the difficulty is solved;—" What the law could not do, in that it was weak through the flesh," was accomplished by the pure and spotless Redeemer who " *died for our sins*," that " by means of" His death all who are called may receive the promise of the eternal inheritance.—1 Cor. xv, 3: Heb. ix, 15. In this way He "*confirmed* the promises," for but for the atoning merits of His death we see not how any one could ever have been made worthy to realize them.

4. The certainty of the promises. The fact that they are the word of the Lord is proof enough of their certainty, but several times it has pleased the Lord to give His word and then confirm it with a solemn oath, thus giving us "two immutable" pledges. "The Lord that *sware* unto me, saying, Unto thy Seed will I give this land."—Gen. xxiv, 7. "I will *perform* the *oath* which I sware unto Abraham thy father."—Gen. xxvi, 3. "I did *swear* to give it to Abraham, to Isaac and to Jacob."—Ex. vi, 8. "Thou wilt perform the truth to Jacob and the mercy to Abraham, which thou hath *sworn* unto our fathers from the days of old."—Mic. vii, 20. Paul in speaking of the promises to Abraham says in the next verse, "The *covenant* that was confirmed before of God in Christ, the law, which was four hundred and thirty years after cannot disannul, that it should make the promise of more effect."—Gal. iii, 17. Here we find that the covenant was "confirmed in Christ," and that the law has never disannulled it. We know by the date also, that he refers to the Abrahamic covenant, for commencing at Sinai, when the law was given, and measuring backwards four hundred and thirty years brings us to NO OTHER period in the world's history but the season when those promises were being made to the fathers. And since those promises were not antiqua-

ted or set aside by the law, and since the office of Christ himself is to "CONFIRM" them, they must remain in full force to this day, or, as Adam Clarke (on Rom. iv) has truly said, "It is the Abrahamic covenant in which we now stand." That is "an *everlasting* covenant," and one of which the Scripture says, "Be ye *always* mindful."—1 Chron. xvi, 17.

5. How may individuals obtain a personal interest in those promises? or, in other words, by what process can they obtain that eternal inheritance and all the ceaseless joys connected with it? This, the most important question of the five, has, perhaps, the easiest and plainest answer. Paul describes the process when he says to some who had submitted to it, "Ye are all the children of God by *faith in Christ Jesus*, for as many of you as have been *baptized into Christ* have put on Christ. . . . And if ye be Christ's *then* are ye Abraham's seed, and heirs according to the promise. . . . Heirs of God and joint heirs with Christ." Gal. iii, 26, 27, 29: Rom. viii, 17. Here are two essential conditions to be complied with before you can become heirs of the promises made to Abraham and his seed. They are, first, "FAITH IN CHRIST JESUS," by which expression Paul, of course, means exactly the *same* as when he told the jailor to "believe on the Lord Jesus Christ."— Ac. xvi, 31. And, as I have shown in a former discourse, no one truly believes on the Lord Jesus,

or has "faith in Christ Jesus," if he refuses to believe the doctrine, message, or testimony which Christ Jesus preached; for "He that hath *received* His testimony hath set to his seal that God is true"; but on the other hand, "He that *believeth not* the Son shall not see life, but the *wrath* of God abideth on him."—John iii, 33, 36. Now the doctrine, message, or testimony which the Son preached was "the gospel of the kingdom of God" (Mark i, 14), and he who truly and affectionately believes that gospel of the kingdom, and sincerely desires to lead a Christian life, is ready to comply with the second condition, which is being "BAPTIZED INTO CHRIST." In duly complying with *both* of those conditions he is enrolled among the "children of God," and becomes "a new creature in Christ Jesus," able to rejoice in the glorious hope of realizing, at the second Advent, his portion in those "exceeding great and precious promises" made unto the fathers.—2 Pet. i, 4.

To recapitulate:—I have now shown, 1st, That, when the Lord Jesus comes in heavenly glory to establish His kingdom, the land of Canaan and the whole earth besides will be given to Him and the redeemed "for an everlasting possession;" 2nd, That this promise of everlasting *possession* involves and carries along with it the additional promise of everlasting *life;* and that the death of Christ for our sins was necessary in order to confirm these promises and make their attainment possible; 3rd,

That a belief of the gospel of the kingdom, and baptism into Christ, followed by holiness of life, are the conditions on which an individual may obtain an inheritance in the promises made unto the fathers.

O then, if you value your own eternal welfare, hasten at once to comply with those terms and conditions. The yoke is easy, the burden light, and the reward surpasses human thought. Come to the Saviour in believing on him and submitting to His appointed ordinance. "Arise and be baptized and wash away thy sins, calling on the name of the Lord."—Ac. xxii, 16. This is a delightful and easy task; not like what was required of Abraham. The command laid upon him was, "Abraham, take now thy son, thine only son Isaac, whom thou lovest, and get thee into the land of Moriah, and offer him there for a burnt-offering upon one of the mountains which I will tell thee of." As Abraham revolved this command in his mind, every clause of it must have pierced like a dagger to his heart. But he did not falter nor seek to change the command and make an offering from his flocks and herds instead. Rising early in the morning he starts on the journey without even telling Sarah of his intentions with regard to the darling of both their hearts. At the prospect of Isaac's birth she had laughed, but she might weep now at the prospect of his death, and so either break her husband's heart or make him waver in the path of duty. Therefore he "consulted not with flesh and blood." God's call is to *you;* do not wait for some one else, but come alone; you have to *die* alone. And now think of Abraham's feelings on that sad journey. Perhaps he said to himself, "O! Isaac, my son Isaac, would to God that I could die *for thee!*" But still he goes forward. And now as they near the fatal spot he lays on Isaac's shoulders the wood on which the offering was first to be slain and then consumed in the fire. Does not this typify that divine Son, the only begotten and dearly beloved, on whose shoulders was laid the very cross on which He was to die? And now comes a thrilling scene, a trying moment. The unresisting Isaac is placed on the altar, and Abraham looks up to heaven with a countenance beaming with angelic faith, and then he raises the great glittering blade and is about to plunge it into the heart of his son, when—hark! a voice rings through the skies, "Abraham! Abraham! lay not thine hand upon the lad, neither do thou anything unto him." And then I can imagine that for the first time in the whole trial his pent-up emotions, too deep for weeping, now find relief in a flood of tears. And looking around he beheld a ram caught in a thicket and offered him up as a substitute for Isaac. But there was no substitute for the Son of God. He endured the great agony himself that we might live. How can you refuse to accept the blood-bought blessings which redeeming love has provided for you?

Do you fear that you will not be accepted if you come to the Saviour? He says "Come unto me *all* ye that labor and are heavy laden, and I will give you rest."—Matthew xi, 28. "There is joy among the angels of God over one sinner that repenteth." Yes,

>Pleased with the news, the saints below
>In songs their tongues employ:
>Beyond the skies the tidings go,
>And heaven is filled with joy.

Suppose a little child wanders from home and is lost in the woods where wild beasts are roaming. Presently the mother and father miss him, and, wringing their hands and weeping, they rush from one neighbor to another, crying out, "Oh! my child is lost! my child is lost!" A general alarm is sounded. Men start out in every direction, some on horses, some afoot. They scatter through the woods and fields in search of the lost one, and at last the almost distracted mother and father, straining their eyes, catch a glad signal of waving handkerchiefs from some distant hill-top that their child is found and safe, and they are coming home with him. Can any words describe the joy with which those loving parents welcome their child back to his home? Neither can words describe the joy felt "over one sinner that repenteth."

FOURTH DISCOURSE.

THE SURE MERCIES; OR, THE COVENANT WITH DAVID.

"'Therefore being a prophet, and knowing that God had sworn with an oath to him, that of the fruit of his loins, according to the flesh, He would raise up Christ to sit on his throne; he seeing this before spake of the resurrection of Christ."—Ac. II, 30, 31.

The great plan of redemption has been gradually unfolded to man. Commencing in Genesis with a few comprehensive sentences it is progressively expanded, as to details, until it shines forth in the apostolic writings as the fully revealed "Gospel of the kingdom." Thus the covenant with David gives a deeper insight into many things that had been mentioned before, especially into that clause of the Abrahamic covenant that speaks of Christ as a great conqueror that "shall possess the gate of His enemies." Of the prominence and importance of this covenant we have sufficient proof in the fact that it is made a *part of the gospel* as proclaimed by Peter in the great Pentecostal sermon. I once met a person who had thought nothing was said of the KINGDOM in that sermon, but confessed being mistaken after attention was called to what it says of David's throne. "The gospel of the kingdom" which Peter was commanded to preach is *composed* of those truths which the Bible reveals concerning that kingdom. How then could Peter or any one else preach the gospel of the kingdom with those truths *left out?* That would be as impossible as to possess the whole of any object without possessing the ingredients or parts of which it is composed; or to have a landscape with the land left out.

We have here but a short memorandum of the principal heads of Peter's discourse, for we are told that he used "many other words," which are not recorded.—Ac. ii, 40. The covenant with David however, being too important a point to be left out, was recorded as a portion of Scripture which " is profitable for doctrine, for reproof, for correction, for instruction in righteousness."—2 Tim. iii, 16. The few but solemn words here recorded about that covenant open the door to all that the Bible says concerning the kingdom of God. Surely the seating of Christ on David's throne must be a matter of profound importance to us all, inasmuch as the Lord hath "sworn with an oath" that it shall be done. To find that oath I turn to 2 Sam. vii, as the marginal reference in my Bible invites me to do. There we find the solemn covenant in these words, " When thy days be fulfilled, and thou shalt sleep with thy fathers, I will set up thy Seed after thee which shall proceed out of thy bowels, and I will establish His kingdom. He shall build an house for my name, and I will establish the throne of His kingdom FOREVER. I will be His

Father, and He shall be my Son. If He commit iniquity, I will chasten Him with the rod of men, and with the stripes of the children of men: but my mercy shall not depart away from Him as I took it away from Saul whom I put away before thee. And thine house and thy kingdom shall be established forever BEFORE THEE: thy throne shall be established FOREVER."

Solomon means peaceable, but that prince in all his glory was but a faint type of the true Prince of peace to whom this covenant points. David in his "last words" referred to this covenant and gave a description of the mighty Ruler to whom it points—a Ruler who had not then appeared in his family; for none but Christ can answer to these descriptions. "He that ruleth over men must be *just* (Christ is '*the Just One*,' Ac. iii, 14), ruling in the *fear of God* (Christ is 'of quick understanding in the fear of the Lord,' Isa. xi, 3). And he shall be as the *light* of the morning when the *sun* riseth (Christ is 'the true light'—'the light of the world'—'the sun of righteousness,' Jno. i, 9; viii, 12; Mal. iv, 2), even as a morning without clouds. Although my house be *not so* with God, yet He hath made with me an *everlasting* covenant, ordered in all things and sure: for this is all my SALVATION and all my DESIRE."—2 Sam. xxiii, 5. Thus he comforted himself "waiting for the kingdom of God." In another place he speaks of the covenant in almost the very words of Peter,

"The Lord hath sworn in truth unto David; He will not turn from it; of the fruit of thy body will I set upon thy throne."—Psa. cxxxii, 11. Words from this covenant are applied to Christ in, Heb. i, 5, as being too high even for angels; of course then they are too high to be restricted to Solomon. As Matthew Henry says, "The establishing of his house, and his throne and his *kingdom forever*, and again and a third time *forever*, can be applied to no other than Christ and his kingdom." It does not say, "He *will* commit," but "*If* he commit iniquity," &c. Adam Clarke translates the clause, "Even in suffering for iniquity I will chasten Him with the rod of men and with the stripes due to the children of Adam;" and refers to Isa. liii, 4, 5. The "house" that He builds will be "a spiritual house" (1 Pet. ii, 5), infinitely superior to the temple made with hands, that Solomon built. House, both in ancient and modern usage frequently means a *family*, as, "come thou and all thy house into the ark."—Gen. vii, 1. "*We* are His house if we hold fast the confidence and the rejoicing of the hope firm unto the *end*."— Heb. iii, 6. The materials are now being selected and polished into shape by the power of the gospel of the kingdom acting on the minds and hearts and lives of those who believe it. The building is not yet completed, for the Scripture does not say, "It *has grown* unto an holy temple," but the process is still going on as indicated by the present tense progressive—"GROWETH unto an holy temple."—Ephes. ii, 21 : iv, 16   It will not be completed until Christ comes.   And indeed prophecy indicates that He will then even cause a literal temple to be built for the millennial age.—Ezekiel XL to XLIII.

☞ That Christ is to possess and reign on the throne of David is a truth affirmed in Scripture too plainly to admit of any doubt. ☜ The Pentecostal sermon alone proves this; but in addition to that are such testimonies as the following : " I have made a covenant with my chosen ; I have sworn unto David, my servant, Thy *seed* will I establish *forever*, and build up thy *throne* to all generations. . . . Once have I sworn by my holiness, that I will not lie unto David. His seed shall *endure forever*, and his throne *as the sun before me*."—Psa. lxxxix, 3, 4, 34-36. " Of this man's (David's) seed hath God, according to *His promise*, raised unto Israel a Saviour, Jesus."—Ac. xiii, 23. " The Lord God shall give unto Him the throne of His father David."—Lu. i, 32, 33. " Of the increase of His government and peace there shall be no end, upon the throne of David, and upon his kingdom, to order it and to establish it with judgment and with justice from henceforth even forever. The zeal of the Lord of Hosts will perform this."—Isa. ix, 7.

Now inasmuch as David has " not ascended into the heavens " (Ac. ii, 34), we know that he has never reigned there; but it is an *historical* truth that he *has* reigned "*in Jerusalem,*" and a *prophetical* truth that Christ *will* hereafter reign "*in Jerusalem.*" You admit the historical part to mean the literal Jerusalem on earth; why not admit the prophetical part to mean the same?— 1 Chron. xxix, 27: Isa. xxiv, 23. If the Czar of Russia were to say to the young Napoleon, "I will give unto thee the throne of thy father, Napoleon III. but come thou up to St. Petersburg and sojourn in my palace until the time comes for the fulfillment of the promise"; people would clearly understand him as meaning that, some of these days, the young Napoleon would be PERSONALLY *enthroned in Paris,* and reign over the French nation and all its colonies. And does not the divine promise that Christ shall be seated on "the throne of His father David" as clearly imply that He must return and be personally enthroned in Jerusalem and reign over the Jewish nation, and over *all* nations and lands throughout the world? Thousands of people would *believe* the Czar, although they would have no stronger reason than the word of a fallible man for their belief. Now, "If we receive the witness of men, the witness of God is greater."—1 John v, 9. The miraculous and literal birth of Christ in Bethlehem, following the prediction by Gabriel of His reign on David's throne, is a sufficient pledge of His literal and miraculous reign in Jerusalem. It is as easy for the Lord to give a perfectly literal fulfillment to the one as to the other prophecy. When Herod in perplexity enquired of the chief priests and scribes where Christ should be born, they gave him a faithful answer:—" In Bethlehem of Judea, for *thus* it is written by the prophet."—Mat. ii, 5. They did not reply in the mystifying, evasive and skeptical style of certain modern teachers, " It is contrary to *our* ideas of the fitness of things to say that He who is to be called ' The Mighty God ' (Isa. ix, 6, 7) can ever be literally born in any literal city on this earth. That seems incongruous. Micah indeed says He will be born in Bethlehem, but we cannot suppose he means the *literal* Bethlehem, about six miles from here, on this very earth, for none but '*an alarmist*' could think such a thing. Our exegesis, which is 'abreast of the times,' has led us to discard the expectation of His birth in a *material* city, and to conclude that the prophet means no more than a *figurative* Bethlehem, whatever that might be; perhaps a city ' beyond the bounds of time and space.' But, in fact, we have never given much attention to the question of ' *Where* shall He be born ? ' For what difference can it make whether it shall be in Bethlehem, or Athens, or even above the skies ? We do not think we ought to be expected to give any *definite* answer to the question of your Royal Highness." It is a notorious fact that the prophecies concerning Messiah's *reign* on earth are treated very much in this way by some who ought to know better.

Listen to a few more testimonies concerning Zion and Jerusalem. "Out of Zion shall go forth the law, and the word of the Lord from Jerusalem." Isa. ii, 3, 4. "At that time they shall call Jerusalem the THRONE of the Lord; and ALL the nations shall be gathered unto it."—Jer. iii, 17. This does not refer to the Mosaic dispensation, for then only the Jewish nation was required to gather there for worship. Nor to the present dispensation, for not even christians are required to go thither now. It must therefore refer to the future or MILLENNIAL dispensation, after the second Advent. Compare Zec. xiv, 4, 5, 16, 17. "And the name of the city from that day shall be THE LORD IS THERE."—Eze. xlviii, 35. "So shall ye know that I am the Lord your God *dwelling in Zion* my holy mountain; then shall Jerusalem be holy, there shall no strangers pass trough her any more." Joel iii, 17. The present overturned condition of the throne of David and city of Jerusalem was in literal fulfillment of prophecy, as also their future restoration will be. When Zedekiah, a "profane and wicked prince," reigned on that throne in Jerusalem the Lord sent this word to him, "I will overturn, overturn, overturn it; and it shall be no more, until He come whose right it is; and I will give it Him."—Eze. xxi, 27. Accordingly, soon after that, the throne of David was overturned, about four hundred and twenty-eight years after Solomon began to reign. And so the Scripture says, "Thou hast made his glory to cease, and cast his throne down to the ground."—Psa. lxxxix, 44. And as to the city and its people, the Saviour predicted before He suffered, "They shall fall by the edge of the sword, and shall be led away captive into all nations; and Jerusalem shall be trodden down of the Gentiles (strangers passing through her, Joel iii, 17), *until* the times of the Gentiles be fulfilled."—Lu. xxi, 24. But it will not remain trodden down, for there shall be a "New Jerusalem . . . and the throne of God and of the Lamb shall be *in it*" as truly as the throne of David was in the old Jerusalem. The heathen who saw the destruction of the old Jerusalem by the Romans perhaps thought they saw the *last* of that city, as when they burned the martyrs they thought they saw the last of *them*. And no doubt many of its captive citizens, led away and sold in foreign lands, "wept when they remembered Zion." She had rejected her Lord, and the glory had departed. And haughty, corrupt Rome, seated on seven hills and insulting the skies with smoke of idol altars, appeared to have nearly the whole world under her sway. But it is *Jerusalem*, not Rome, Ninevah, Washington or London, that the Lord has "graven on the palms of His hands."—Isa. xlix, 16. And John who had walked in the streets of the old city, and lived to know of her destruction, was comforted by a prophetic and rapturous view of the *new* Jerusalem, having the glory of God, and into which no Judas, nor Pilate, nor Herod, nor Caiaphas can enter, but only "they which are written in the Lamb's book of life."—Rev. xxi, 2, 11, 27; xxii, 3. Two great prophetic periods are limited by the word "until," and will end together. They are, 1st, The personal absence of Christ in heaven "UNTIL the times of restitution" or restoration. 2nd, The down-treading of Jerusalem "UNTIL the times of the Gentiles be fulfilled." They will end when the Lord Jesus shall personally "*return* and build again the tabernacle of David that is fallen down." "When the Lord shall build up Zion, He shall appear in His glory."—Ac. xv, 16; Psa. cii, 16.

The Saviour is now seated on His Father's throne, but while there speaks of *another*—His own—on which he will take His seat when He returns to the earth. We learn this from His two sayings, "To him that overcometh will I grant to sit with me on *my* throne, even as I also overcame and am set down with my Father on *His* throne." Rev. iii, 21; and "When the Son of man shall *come* in His glory, and all the holy angels with Him, *then* shall He sit upon the throne of His glory," or "His throne of glory," as the American Bible Union renders it; or "His glorious throne,"—Campbell's edition. The fact that He *comes* to take His seat on it proves that His throne will be on earth; for if it were in heaven His coming here would be *leaving* it instead of *coming to* it.

Those words of the covenant, "Thy kingdom shall be established forever *before* thee" are explained by the similar promise that "The Lord of hosts shall reign in mount Zion and in Jerusalem, and before His ancients gloriously."—Isa. xxiii, 24. In the Greek it is the same word, *enōpion*, in both places, and means "in the presence of," it being so rendered in many places, as for instance, "I am Gabriel that stand (*enōpion*) in the presence of God."—Lu. 1, 19. "Many other signs truly did Jesus (*enōpion*) in the presence of His disciples."—Jno. xx, 30. Hence the promise to David meant the privilege of being "ever with the Lord" in His "everlasting kingdom."—2 Pet. i, 11. And this justifies David's remarkable saying that the covenant was "all of his *salvation* and all of his *desire*."—2 Sam. xxiii, 5. The eternal blessings involved in that promise are "the sure mercies of David." But these mercies are not for David exclusively, for the promise to *all* believers is "I will give to *you* the sure mercies of David."— Ac. xiii, 34. The pronoun "you" (Greek, *humin*) is *plural* here, as usual in King James' version the singular being thee or thou, and means that all believers are joint-heirs with Christ of the *royalty* promised in this covenant, as they are of the inheritance promised in the Abrahamic covenant. The following are some of the testimonies concerning the future royal honors of the redeemed: "To him that overcometh will I grant to sit with me in my throne."—Rev. iii, 21. "If we suffer, we shall also reign with him."—2 Tim. ii, 12. "Then shall the King say unto them on His right hand, come ye blessed of my Father, inherit the kingdom."—Mat. xxv, 34. "A *King* shall reign in righteousness and *princes* shall rule in judgment."—Isa. xxxii, 1. "It is your Father's good pleasure to give to you the kingdom."—Lu. xii, 32. "The kingdom and dominion, and the greatness of the kingdom under the whole heaven shall be given to the people of the saints of the Most High."—Dan. vii, 27. "They lived and reigned with Christ a thousand years."—Rev. xx, 4. "Thou wast slain, and hast redeemed to God by thy blood out of every kindred, and tongue, and people, and nation; and hast made us unto our God kings and priests; and we shall reign *on the earth*."—Rev. v, 10. It is not we did or do reign, but "we *shall* reign"—it is *future*. That future relationship which Christ will sustain to the church is represented under the beautiful similitude of a royal Bridegroom and His Bride, endowed by Him with queenly honors, and seated with Him on His throne."—Psa. xlv; Mat. xxv, 10; Rev. xix, 7; xxi, 2, 9.

But the Lord Jesus did not obtain the throne of David and reign in Jerusalem at His first coming. The wicked persons then usurping authority in that city rejected Him; as indicated by such expressions as, "We will not have this man to reign over us. . . . This is the heir, come let us kill him. . . . We have no king but Cæsar."—Mat. xxi, 38: Lu. xix, 14; Jno. xix, 15. And so, after they had crucified Him, He arose from the dead and ascended into heaven, without obtaining possession either of the covenanted *land*, or of the covenanted *throne*. But He holds the title-deeds to both, and His claims are just as good and fresh to-day as they ever were. The enmity and wrath of man cannot possibly defeat the immutable decrees of Him who maketh the wrath of man praise Him, and restraineth the remainder of wrath. The church is therefore not to lose faith in the promises. Her Lord has left her with the blessed and comforting assurance of His literal and personal *return*—" this *same* Jesus which is taken up from you into heaven, shall *so* come in *like manner*."—Ac. i, 11. "The Lord HIMSELF shall descend from heaven with a shout, with the voice of the archangel, and the trump of God; and the dead in Christ shall rise."—1 Thes. iv, 16. We see then that He has never relinquished His claims but will certainly enforce them all at His return; for He himself has assured us that "*when* the Son of man shall COME in His *glory*, and all the holy angels with Him, THEN shall He sit upon the throne of His glory."—Mat. xxv, 31. Then, with the land of Canaan as a nucleus and Jerusalem as a capital, His dominion shall by miraculous judgments break in pieces all other kingdoms, and extend "from sea even to sea; and from the river to the ends of the earth."—Dan. ii, 35, 44: Zec. ix, 10. For the king then seated on the "holy hill of Zion" shall have, not Canaan only, but "the *uttermost parts* of the earth for His possession."—Psa. ii, 6, 8.

The two "covenants of promise"—one with Abraham and the other with David—centre in Christ the great Heir. I have now explained those covenants to you, and have shown that all christians have a direct and personal interest in both of them. But what was their condition before obtaining that interest? Let Paul answer,—"At that time ye were without Christ, being aliens from the commonwealth of Israel, and *strangers* from the covenants of promise, having *no hope*, and without God in the world."—Ephes. ii, 12. There are two ways of being a stranger from a will or covenant:—1st, As to *information* concerning it. Such a person knows neither what benefits are offered in it, nor the terms on which they are offered. Persons of accountability (i. e. ability to give account) who are in this condition with regard to the "covenants of promise" are in danger of being "destroyed for lack of *knowledge;*" being "alienated from the life of God through the *ignorance* that is in them."—Hos. iv, 6: Ephes. iv, 18. But, 2nd, a man may be well acquainted with the reading of a will or covenant without having one particle of *personal* interest or share in it, merely on account of not having complied with its *terms*. His name not being in the document, he is, as far as personal interest is concerned, still an alien and stranger to it; and has no right to expect any benefit from it. And so with regard to the covenants of promise; you may understand and believe them and yet remain a stranger from them simply by refusing to comply with the specified terms or conditions on which one is made an heir. In other words, you may believe the glorious gospel of the kingdom—of which those covenants form the *main outlines*—and yet if you refuse to be baptized for the remission of sins, and to have your name enrolled in the Lamb's book of life you still remain an alien and a stranger from the covenants, "having no *hope*."

You must admit the first and second propositions of the following plain syllogism, and admitting them to be true, you must admit the third as a necessary consequence—1: You cannot be saved if you refuse to believe *that* gospel which Christ and His apostles preached. 2: *They* preached the gospel of the kingdom. 3: *Therefore* you cannot be saved if you refuse to believe the gospel of the kingdom. Must we then believe that so many benevolent people and so many eloquent preachers will have to believe the gospel of the kingdom and be baptized for the remission of sins before they can be saved! Why not? We ought to be perfectly willing to believe *anything* that God's word says to us. I suppose that none of those preachers are more "eloquent," or more "mighty in the Scriptures," or more "fervent in the spirit," or more "diligently" devoted to their work than Apollos: and yet even he needed to have "expounded unto him the way of God more perfectly," by two humble believers of the gospel of the kingdom.—Ac. xviii, 24, 26. I suppose that none of those benevolent people excel Cornelius. He was "A devout man, and one that feared God with all his house, which gave much alms to the people, and prayed to God always. A just man, and of good report among all the nation of the Jews." And yet, notwithstanding all these excellencies, he "was *warned* from God," yes, "*warned*," to send for a preacher of the gospel of the kingdom, and to hear from him words whereby he might "be saved," and after hearing those words he had to "be *baptized*."—Ac. x, 1, 2, 22, 48: xi, 14. To the question, "What shall we do?" Peter replied, "Repent and be baptized every one of you in the name of Jesus Christ for the remission of sins."— Ac. ii, 38. And here let me ask every candid person, If all the people now living on the earth, together with all who have lived since the day of Pentecost had been there in Peter's presence that day, can you suppose that he would have altered his answer in the slightest particular for the sake of complying with their notions, partialities, or prejudices? Not in one jot or tittle would he have altered or compromised it, for it is the word which God commanded him to speak.

It is a gospel repentance—a "*repentance unto life*"—which is here required.*—Ac. xi, 18. Such a repentance does not stop with merely being sorry for sins committed: nor even with forming a resolution to forsake them; but is an actual "ceasing to do evil and learning to do well."—Isa. i, 16, 17. *Testimony* on any subject must, of course, precede belief or *faith* in what is testified: that belief or faith must precede any *feeling* in correspondence with the truths testified: and that feeling must precede *action* in conformity to it. *Testimony, faith, feeling, action* are therefore seen to be bound together by a natural and gracious necessity. And will not every Bible-student say that when a person HEARS the gospel of the kingdom, BELIEVES it, and FEELS and ACTS according to the truths which it contains and the duties which it enjoins,—such a person has "become a new creature in Christ Jesus,"

---

* *Metanoeo* (*repent*), "To perceive or come to a conviction afterwards; to change one's mind or purpose; to repent." *Metanoia* (repentance), "After-thought; a change of mind on reflection: hence repentance."—So these two words are defined in Lexicon of Liddell & Scott. "Repentance is strictly a change of mind, and includes the whole of that alteration with respect to views, disposition, and conduct, which is affected by the power of the gospel."—Edwards' Encyclopedia.

and has undergone that change of heart and life which is an evidence of true conversion to God?

And now will *you* walk in this pathway? Will you believe and feel and act as the gospel requires, and thus obtain an eternal inheritance in the kingdom at last? Unless you obtain that inheritance you will not be saved. This is God's plan of saving people. Rest assured then that if saved at all, you will be saved in *that* kingdom which He will establish on earth at the second coming of Christ. God has proved His pardoning love in giving His only begotten Son to die for you. No "mourner's bench," with agonizing prayer and weeping is now needed to secure His mercy. The mourning and agony were endured by the holy Saviour in the lonely vale of Gethsemane, and on the bloody steep of Calvary. " Surely *He* hath borne our griefs and carried our sorrows."—Isa. liii, 4. Have you faith in *His* tears, *His* prayers, and *His* intercession? if so come just as you are, with a heart filled with love to Jesus and faith in His word. " Him that cometh unto me I will in *no wise* cast out." When the prodigal son "came to himself" he said " I will arise and go to my Father." These words—came to himself—show that sin is a madness; the the sinner is out of his mind! beside himself! It seems to me that if any sinner could have one lucid interval, one sweet, calm, hour of returning reason his eyes would be opened; he would see his surroundings, and would flee from sin with more horror than from the deadliest plague or pestilence.

Let me say to all who are walking in the bright and rosy path of the morning of life, 'twill save you from a thousand snares to mind religion young. "Remember *now* thy Creator, in the days of thy youth."—Eccl. xii, 1. Beware of that pernicious notion that you ought to "sow your wild oats;" it has been the destruction of thousands who have seen their error when it was *too late*; and so, with habits of evil fixed upon them like leopard spots that could not be changed, they have sunk down into the sinner's grave—lost, lost, lost. You may be sure that Samuel and Timothy sowed no wild oats, for the latter from a child, knew the Holy Scriptures; and "Samuel ministered before the Lord, being a child, girded with a linen ephod." But the brightest and best instance of all was the holy Redeemer, who, in childhood as in later years, left an example for mankind. As early as twelve years of age He was found in the great Temple at Jerusalem saying, "Wist ye not that I must be about my Father's business?"

Parents, if you have sons and daughters who believe the gospel of the kingdom, speak to them about the importance of coming *now* and dedicating their young lives to God "in a perpetual covenant that shall not be forgotten." You see their danger while they remain out of the ark of safety; does it not distress you to know that the children of your love are the children of God's wrath? Do not encourage them in worldliness under the notion that in due time they will forsake such things and be all the better for the experience. This would be doing evil that good may come: a principle positively condemned by Scripture. Would you not think a physician utterly insane who would take a patient only a *little* ailing, and send him off to a "Pest House" among fevers and epidemics, to contract all its contagions before administering any remedy? What if the fearful experiment be carried *too far!* and the patient *die*, instead of coming out of it all and enjoying better health than ever before! How broad and comprehensive, yet how tender and eloquent is that exhortation to Christian parents concerning their children,— "Bring them up in the *nurture and admonition* of the Lord."—Ephes. vi, 4. It does not teach you to bring them up wrong, hoping they will soon go right; but to bring them up right, hoping they will *never* go wrong.

There is no excuse for *any* one to remain out of the ark of safety. The door of salvation is open to *you*, whether old or young, rich or poor. What you have to do may be told in a few words,—believe the joyful tidings that Christ is coming soon to establish His glorious and blissful kingdom on earth, and that through the merits of His precious blood you may obtain endless life and happiness in that kingdom "at the resurrection of the just." This, expressed as it were in a nutshell, is "the gospel of the kingdom." Believe this gospel, then be baptized for the remission of sins, thenceforth continue "faithful unto death;" and you will surely be saved when the Redeemer comes. No "mourners' bench" in all this arrangement. That bench and the process carried on at it are contrary to the free grace of the gospel. Some have gone away from such a bench under the desponding impression that religion was not for them, and so their last condition became worse than the first. When the prodigal son said, "I will arise and go to my father," did he have to fall down at the door and go through a mourners'-bench process— weeping, screaming, and getting some of the old neighbors to come and link their petitions with his—in order to get his father reconciled? No; but "when he was yet a *great* way off, his father saw him, and had *compassion*, and *ran*, and fell on his neck, and *kissed* him, and said to his servants, Bring forth the *best* robe, and put it on him, and put a *ring* on his hand, and *shoes* on his feet; and bring hither the *fatted calf*, and kill it, and let us *eat and be merry;* for this my son was dead and is alive again; he was lost and is found." What a thrilling parable is this! full of meat for men, and milk for babes. Plain enough for a child to understand it, and yet profoundly describing the depths of God's mercy! How it would mar and jar the whole parable to pieces to crowd into it such an incongruous and unscriptural thing as a modern mourner's bench! Christ is the One Mediator who has prepared the way for the sinner's return—"God was IN CHRIST reconciling the world unto himself."—2 Cor. v, 19. No one then ought to imagine himself rejected, but all ought to gladly ACCEPT the freely-offered salvation, as on the day of Pentecost "they *gladly* received the word." Pardon is not only freely offered to but warmly urged upon even the vilest of sinners, for when Peter was preaching to those who "by wicked hands had crucified and slain the Saviour," he "testified and exhorted" with many words, saying, "Save yourselves from this untoward generation."—Ac. ii, 23, 40. The word here translated "exhort" (*parakaleo*) is a very strong one, and means, according to Greenfield's Lexicon, "To call upon, invite, exhort, admonish, persuade, beg, beseech, entreat, implore." It is used to describe the fervent entreaty of Jairus for his daughter, and is there translated "besought."— Lu. viii, 41. It is a duty enjoined upon those who preach the gospel—"reprove, rebuke, *exhort*," *parakaleo.*—2 Tim. iv, 2. And there is a sufficient cause for all this fervid exhortation; your eternal welfare depends on your accepting the offered salvation. "How shall we escape if we neglect so great salvation?"—Heb ii, 3.

Sinner, how can you find any enjoyment or have one peaceful hour so long as your name is not in the Book of Life? I wonder you are not startled from sleep at the midnight hour with those fearful words ringing in your ears:—"*Whosoever* was not found written in the book of life was cast into *the lake of fire.*"—Rev. xx, 15. What a sweeping word is that whosoever! There are two great whosoevers in the Bible—this, describing the coming doom of the wicked; and the other pointing to the only door of escape;—"God so loved the world that He gave His only begotten Son, that WHOSOEVER believeth in Him should not perish, but have everlasting life."—John iii, 16. Will you now believe in Him, so that in the resurrection you may obtain that life and all the blessings pertaining thereto?

FIFTH DISCOURSE.

THE ETERNAL INHERITANCE.

"And for this cause He is the Mediator of the New Testament, that *by means of death*, for the redemption of the transgressions that were under the first Testament, they which are called might receive the promise of *the (tes) eternal* inheritance."—HEB. IX, 15.

Somewhere in the universe the righteous will obtain what the Scriptures call "An heavenly *country*," Heb. xi, 16; "An inheritance among them that are *sanctified*," Ac. xxvi, 18; "The inheritance of the saints *in light*," Col. i, 12; "The land of *the promise*," Heb. xi, 9; "The *eternal* inheritance." In the present state men soon die and leave their wealth to others. No human law can write such a deed to a piece of property as will secure its owner from death. The lease hardly goes beyond threescore years and ten. But that future inheritance will be "forever," "eternal." Psa. xxxvii, 18. Another precious thought is, it will be "*in light.*" We quickly feel the depressing effects of a dark and murky atmosphere, or the animating influence of bright and balmy weather. "Truly the light is *sweet.*"—Eccl. xi, 7. It is sometimes used as a symbol of joy. "Light is sown for the righteous, and gladness for the upright in heart."—Psa. xcvii, 11. Imagine if you can what a gloomy abode the earth would be were we deprived of the present measure of light which the Lord has commanded to shine upon it. (There will be a sevenfold increase of that light if Isa. xxx, 26, is to be taken literally.) A third feature serving to render that inheritance of inestimable value is that it will be "among them that are *sanctified.*" It is well known what effect the neighbors have on the value of a piece of land. Men will pay a large price for a lot or farm in a *good* neighborhood, who would regard it a great calamity to have to reside on the same piece of land surrounded by *bad* neighbors. Well, in this respect the future inheritance will be all that heart can wish. The society will excel anything that the mind of mortal man can imagine. A fourth very important and essential feature is that it will be a "*country*," a "*land*," a real and *tangible* abode for beings with tangible, immortal, and glorified bodies like their Lord. "The righteous shall inherit *substance*."—Prov. viii, 21. I cannot imagine how there could be tangible resurrected bodies without any tangible pedestal or territory to rest upon. After creating Adam and Eve the Lord did not throw them off into space to float forever as mere atoms in the air, but gave them a beautiful and tangible territory to dwell upon. The resurrection of the Saviour proves that His redeemed will have tangible bodies, for they "shall be like Him," shall "bear His image," and have their bodies "fashioned like unto His own glorious body."—1 John iii, 2; 1 Cor. xv, 49; Phil. iii, 21. That glorious fashion will never become old, but will have the stamp of immortality fixed upon it. Some giddy people have said, "Better be out of the world than out of the fashion"; but they had indeed better be out of the world, yes, better never have come into the world than to be kept out of *that* fashion when the Saviour comes.

I have met persons who cry out against "materiality," when at the same time they are utterly unable to tell us either where materiality ends, or where their favorite "immateriality" begins. In denying the tangibility of the future existence they have denied the tangible resurrection of the body, and thus have lost themselves in the cold, murky and shoreless ocean of speculation. But "the disciple whom Jesus loved" was not of that school, for he has described to us a Saviour whom his "hands had handled," and they did even "eat and drink with Him *after* He rose from the dead." 1 John i, 1: Ac. x, 41. The Saviour had foretold that he would be crucified and raised again the third day, and had even given visible evidence of the resurrection of the body, in raising the ruler's daughter, the widow's son, and Lazarus. But still Thomas doubted the real and tangible resurrection of his Lord. Perhaps he was tainted with something like the modern mysticism, and insisted on a *figurative* interpretation. Before he could believe in the *literal* fulfillment of the Saviour's prophecy he must "see in His hands the print of the nails, and put his finger into the print of the nails, and thrust his hand into His side." Well, whatever false theory had beclouded the mind of Thomas, his conversion was thorough. When permitted to see for himself he did not cry out, "This is too literal, this is too material; I'll have nothing to do with it." No; but from the depths of his heart he says, "My Lord and my God." In his estimation, the Saviour's *tangibility* did not *lessen His divinity.*—John xx, 25–28.

In the resurrected and "spiritual body" there will be infinitely more *reality* than in this "mortal body" which "appeareth for a little time and then vanisheth away."—Jas. iv, 14. We may conjecture that the perishable blood, which is the life of the present flesh (Deut. xii, 23), will be superceded by the imperishable Spirit in the future constitution; so that the body will then be "flesh and bones," but not "flesh and blood." This will make the glory and beauty of the spiritual body infinitely excel that of the mortal body. According to Chemistry, carbon is the basis of charcoal, and the Diamond is pure carbon, or charcoal changed, crystalized, glorified. So the spiritual body will be the present humble body "changed," immortalized, glorified. I have read of a Jacinth no larger than a pea, but which is said to flash and glow with a lustre that seems to indicate the presence of fire and flame. Even the sun and stars are used to illustrate the future glory of the redeemed.— Dan. xii, 3 : Mat. xiii, 43. So we may well believe that the resurrection body will be stronger than the Diamond, more beautiful than the Jacinth, and bright as the stars or sun; yet without blood.

As already intimated, a great community of such beings must have a tangible abode; something must be some *where*. On a clear night you can see a great many stars in the sky; with a telescope you could see more; and with *perfect* vision perhaps the whole sky would seem one silvery surface of star-work, without a single blue interspace. But could you point to a single spot in that star-work and say, on Scriptural authority, "*That* shall be forever the saints' secure abode?" Let us then consider *where* will the inheritance be? when will it be obtained? and by what means.

1. *Where* will the inheritance be? This and the other two questions are explained under the similitude of a Testament or covenant promising a certain inheritance to certain heirs. The fact that the word translated "testament," (*diathēke*), means also a "covenant" produces no obscurity in the text but rather brings out the meaning more clearly; because the testament or will referred to contains within itself the nature of a covenant also, inasmuch as although it is brought into force by a *death* (like a will), yet its bequests are to be given to the heirs on conditions which (as in a covenant), must be *agreed to and complied with* by them. And now to find the inheritance for which we are looking we must first find the testament or covenant in which it is described. Paul mentions two testaments—the Abrahamic and Mosaic. The latter he calls "the *first* testament" because though the last made it was the first that was brought into force.—Heb. ix, 18. He also calls it "the *old* testament" because in his time it had become old and "ready to vanish away."—2 Cor. iii, 14; Heb. viii, 13. It is only in a loose or metonymic way that we speak of all the books from Genesis to Malachi as "The Old Testament." That volume *contains* "The Old Testament" i. e. it contains Exodus, Leviticus, Numbers and Deuteronomy, in

which the old testament or Mosaic covenant was written. It also contains the "prophets," to whom we are still commanded to "take heed," (2 Pet. i, 19); but we are forbidden to put ourselves under the Mosaic law. We must therefore distinguish between "the *law* and the *prophets*." Now if we search the Mosaic testament with all eagerness we shall never find our eternal inheritance *there*. That testament has indeed shown us a nation settled upon a land; but at the same time it warned them that they were but "strangers and sojourners" i. e. *temporary* residents upon it.—L v. xxv, 23. Accordingly, as their history proves, they "possessed it but a *little while*."—Isa. lxiii, 18. An eternal inheritance requires eternal *life* as a qualification for it. But the Mosaic testament could not give that eternal life because it could not give *righteousness*, of which that life is the reward; hence the eternal inheritance came not by the law of Moses. In this argument Paul clearly affirms that none but the righteous can obtain eternal life, and none but those who have eternal life can obtain the eternal inheritance. "As *righteousness* tendeth to *life*: so he that pursueth *evil* pursueth it to his own *death*"—Prov. xi. 19. "The wages of sin is death, but the gift of God is eternal life through our Lord Jesus Christ."—Rom. vi, 23; Gal. iii, 21; ii, 21.

Having shown that the Mosaic testament or covenant did not give an eternal inheritance, let us now turn to the Abrahamic testament or covenant.

This is called "the *new* testament" as distinguished from the Mosaic, because it is "*everlasting;*" for what is everlasting must be *always* new; and will never become old and vanish away, as did the Mosaic. The effects of this new covenant must remain as long as the redeemed and their inheritance exist. It is also "new" because although typically confirmed four hundred and thirty years before the law it was not antitypically or fully confirmed until about fifteen hundred years *after* the law, when the blood of Christ was shed as "the blood of the *everlasting* covenant," and thus a different, "a *new* and *living* way," was opened up for the pardon of sin; a way new and different from any that had been seen before, whether under the Mosaic or the patriarchal dispensation.—Heb. xiii, 20: x, 20.

The following reasons prove that it is the Abrahamic covenant in which all Christians now stand, and hence the inheritance promised in that covenant is theirs: 1st, The law could not disannul it, Gal. iii, 17. 2nd, Christ came "to confirm" its promises, Rom. xv, 8. 3rd, He is the one Seed named in that covenant and therefore the Heir, while they are the multitudinous seed and joint-heirs with Him of the *same* inheritance.—Gal. iii, 16, 29: Rom. viii, 17. 4th, It is "an everlasting covenant," and therefore still in force. —Gen. xvii, 7, 8: 1 Chron. xvi, 15–18.

Paul says this new covenant, of which Christ is Mediator, is "better" than the Mosaic, and was "established upon better promises."—Heb. viii, 6. Let us contrast them in a few particulars.— Moses was mediator of the Mosaic covenant: but Christ is Mediator of the Abrahamic. The Mosaic was dedicated by blood of calves and goats "which can never take away sin:" but the Abrahamic by the precious blood of Christ which "cleanseth us from all sin."—1 Jno. i, 7. The Mosaic covenant was only provisional or temporary—till Christ should come: but the Abrahamic is everlasting.—Gal. iii, 19. The Mosaic covenant could not confer righteousness, eternal life, nor the eternal heritance: but the Abrahamic confers all these on its heirs. The Mosaic bequeathed chiefly to one nation: the Abrahamic bequeaths to believers of *all* nations.

All these considerations with regard to the two covenants prove conclusively that it is the Abrahamic covenant in which we must find the eternal inheritance pointed out. Paul says, "To Abraham and his Seed were the promises made. He saith not And to seeds, as of many, but as of one, And to thy Seed, which is Christ. And this I say, that the covenant, that was confirmed before of God in Christ, the law, which was four hundred and thirty years after, cannot disannul that it should make the promise of none effect. For if the inheritance be of the law, it is no more of promise."—Gal. iii, 16-18. In this brief quotation is condensed a rich treasury of wisdom. Among other things, it tells us that the INHERITANCE is the thing promised; that Abraham and his Seed (i. e. Christ and the saints, ver 20) are the heirs; and that these promises, also called a *"covenant,"* were made four hundred and thirty years before the law. Now, commencing with the giving of the law at Sinai, and measuring backwards four hundred and thirty years, we come to the days when the covenant was being made, and we hear the Lord promising to give *an eternal inheritance* to Abraham and his Seed. In such expressions as the following the promise is several times repeated—" Unto thy Seed will I give *this* land."— Gen. xii, 7. " All the land which thou seest, to thee will I give it, and to thy Seed *forever."*—Gen. xiii, 15. " I will give unto thee, and to thy Seed after thee, the land wherein thou art a stranger, all the land of Canaan for an *everlasting* possession." Gen. xvii, 8. Nor is this all of the inheritance, for when Christ and His joint-heirs take possession of that land the kingdom of God will be established there and will quickly fill the "*whole* earth ;" hence another promise of Scripture says that Christ shall have " the *uttermost parts* of the earth for His possession ;" and another, " Blessed are the meek for *they* shall inherit the earth."—Dan. ii, 35 : Psa. ii, 8 : Mat. v, 5.

We have now proved, 1st, That the Abrahamic covenant is " the *new* testament " spoken of in the text; 2nd, That Christ is the Heir and all the righteous joint-heirs with Him; 3rd, That the land of Canaan and the *whole earth* will be their "eternal inheritance."

Some, although they cannot deny this plain conclusion, try to avoid confessing that the earth is to be our future inheritance by saying they do not think it "*essential*" to believe it. But this undertaking to sit in judgment on Holy Scripture, and divide off its truths into essential and non-essential is a presumptuous and perilous affair. What would you think of a man who, trying to reduce faith and morals to the utmost *minimum*—to a mere skeleton—would undertake to form for himself a creed and a moral code omitting every truth and every grace or virtue except what he might deem "absolutely essential" to his final salvation? Do you think a character based on such a creed and such a code as that would be approved in the day of judgment, or that such a man would be saved at all? To suppress the many precious promises which declare the whereabouts of the inheritance is like impiously trying to run a pen through those promises, or to hide their light under a bushel. The Lord has not revealed anything superfluous; "*whatsoever* things were written aforetime were written for our learning."—Rom. xv, 4. "All Scripture is profitable for *doctrine*."—2 Tim. iii, 16. We should gladly accept "every word that proceedeth out of the mouth of God."—Mat. iv, 4. The whereabouts of the inheritance is a prominent part of that gospel of the kingdom which we must believe in order to be saved. Compare Mat. xxiv, 14; Mar. xvi, 16. The Lord has told us where the inheritance will be, and has sworn to perform His promise—" I will *perform* the oath which I sware unto Abraham,"—(Gen. xxvi, 3); surely then it is essential to believe that He will keep His word. The blessed Son of God has also told us where it will be, saying, " blessed are the meek for they shall inherit *the earth* "—(Mat. v, 5); and it is essential to believe Him also, for " He that believeth not the Son shall not see life; but the wrath of God abideth on him."—Jno. iii, 36.

Common sense teaches us that in taking a journey to any place we are much more apt to get there and will have a much easier journey if we know just where it is before we start; otherwise we are liable to go in an opposite direction, and perhaps never get there. Does an attorney in writing a deed of great importance think it non-essential to specify the whereabouts of the estate conveyed? In the parables of the supper and the marriage feast—(Lu. xiv; Mat. xxii), suppose you that the servants who carried the invitations neglected to tell the invited ones *where* the supper or feast would be? Is it customary to leave out such an important item as that? Well, the servants in those parables represent those who preach " the gospel of the kingdom," by which gospel the Lord is inviting us to " His kingdom and glory." And truly that gospel tells us plainly enough *where* the kingdom and glory will be. These are " things which are *revealed* " and therefore " belong unto us and to our children forever."—Deut. xxix, 29.

2. When will the inheritance be obtained? "A testament is of force *after* men are dead; otherwise it is of no strength at all while the testator liveth."--Heb. ix, 17. And in some instances an estate is not received until a *long time after* the testator's death, owing to the non-age of some of the heirs. But was it ever known in any court of law since the world began, that a portion of the heirs, not only during the non-age of some but also before the birth of some, and even before the death of the testator were put in possession of the inheritance? Now whether we call the arrangement alluded to in the text a testament or only a covenant, there can be no disputing the fact that it required the death of Christ to bring it into *force*. How then could those heirs who died *before* the Testator obtain immediately that inheritance; entering into possession of an heavenly Canaan at death, as some people tell us? Would not this be utterly subversive of the testamentary illustration? Why speak of the eternal inheritance as something to be obtained *by and after* the death of Christ if it could be equally obtained without and before His death? This very epistle to the Hebrews declares that those who died before the death of Christ " received not the promise,"

and shall "not be made perfect without us."—Heb. xi, 39, 40. After Abraham, Isaac and Jacob had been dead nearly two hundred years the giving of the inheritance to them was spoken of as still *future*.—Ex. vi, 4. *All* the heirs will receive it together, at the resurrection, as many lines of argument converge to prove. Some of those lines of argument are, (1) those testimonies which mention particular heirs; (2) those which describe the present condition of the inheritance; (3) those relating to the state of the dead; (4) the great parables.

Abraham obtained "none inheritance in it," and the great Redeemer himself even while sojourning upon it "had not where to lay his head." Ac. vii, 5; Mat. viii, 20. But when He shall "come in His glory" He will receive "the uttermost parts of the earth" for his possession.---Psa. ii, 8.

The inheritance itself had yet to be prepared even for the *apostles*; how then could the patriarchal heirs who died during the previous four thousand years be already in it? If the patriarchs were already in it, and it was good enough for them, was it not good enough for the apostles? But how can you suppose that the Saviour speaks of the holy heaven above as the place to be prepared? Since it is already good enough for the Father, the Son, the Holy Spirit and the holy angels, I would think that we ought rather to be prepared for that, than that for us. But it is evident that the groaning *earth*, waiting to be delivered shall indeed be prepared and repaired by Him who will "make all things new."---Rev. xxi, 5; Rom. viii, 21.* The regenerated earth which the meek shall inherit (Mat. v, 5) after thus prepared, will be as homogeneous with their risen and glorified bodies as the present earth is with their present bodies. The Saviour's going to heaven has much to do with the making ready or preparing of that inheritance; and we must wait until He shall "*come again*" and receive us to himself, before we can enter into possession of it. The present state of the dead proves they will not obtain it before the resurrection. They "know not anything"—Eccles. ix, 5. "The grave is their house"—Job xvii, 13. They "sleep in the dust of the earth"—Dan. xii, 2. Have "not ascended into heaven"—Ac. ii, 34. They "shall be recompensed at the *resurrection* of the just"—(Lu. xiv, 14), "when the Son of man shall come in the glory of His Father with His angels—(Mat. xvi, 27), and when they shall put on the prerequisite immortality."—1 Cor. xv, 54.

---

* "God intends to rescue the creation from this confused state, and to deliver it from being thus held in bondage to man's depravity, that it may partake of and minister to the glorious liberty of His children."—SCOTT, *on Rom. viii.* "The whole earth shall become a more beautiful paradise than Adam ever saw."—JOHN WESLEY, *in sermon on the New Creation.*

The great parables prove the same. The laborers in the vineyard were employed at different hours during the day, but paid off at one stated season, " when *evening* was come." We must be content to go by the Master's clock; our times are in His hand. When the great dial-plate above that marks the times and seasons points to the hour of His return, He will come without delay and call the laborers, from " the last " that entered the vineyard and are still toiling above the sod, to " the first " who entered it long ago and are now sleeping in the silent grave. " Thou shalt call, and I will answer thee," says Job. Yes, from land and ocean He will summon them—" gather my saints together unto me; those that have made a covenant with me by sacrifice," even by the great Sacrifice on Calvary. How beautifully the parable fits with calling persons into the Church all through the past ages and dispensations, and rewarding them all together at the resurrection when the Lord comes! And just as the laborers are not paid off irregularly through the day, as if the steward were kept in his office constantly employing one and paying another; so neither are the wheat and tares gathered singly and at odd times all through the year, but in the time of *harvest*, at the *end* of the age," *aiōn*. Also the good fish and bad are represented as arraigned and separated in a multitude, when the net is *full* and brought to shore; not one by one, every few minutes, as by a hook and line process. Thus with wonderful clearness these parables teach that the righteous are not singly and every day going from some part or other of the "field" or "vineyard" or "sea" immediately to glory—though we hear in some funeral sermons that the deceased has "gone to his reward"—but must wait and "be recompensed at the *resurrection* of the just," not at the *death* of the just.—Luke xiv, 14. The attitude of those who have turned to God is that of "waiting for His Son from heaven."—1 Thes. i, 10. Even the righteous dead may be spoken of as waiting for Him, for Job says, "All the days of my appointed time will I wait till my change come," and "If I wait the grave is my house."—Job xiv, 14: xvii, 13. And so they have only, as it were, changed waiting-rooms—they in the grave, we in the world. I have been told that some of the early Christians, to express their faith, were buried in a standing posture as if anxiously "gazing up into heaven" (like the disciples on Olivet), "not having received the promises," but waiting for the returning Saviour.

The Church has waited long and suffered much during the heavenly Bridegroom's absence in the "far country" to which He has gone; and what if in the very act of returning some angelic band were to meet Him in the skies and say, "She is even now *dead,* for the last Christian on earth has been put to death by persecution," would even that cause Him to turn back? An earthly physician, if met on the way by tidings that his patient is dead, turns back and goes to struggle with death and be again defeated on some other battle-field. But Oh! it is not so with Christ, the great physician. Such tidings would but hasten him hither, for He could say, as He did of the ruler's daughter, "*She is not dead but sleepeth.*" And on His arrival, His bright presence will throw a stream of light into the deepest grave of His people, and His sweet voice awaken all their dust into life and everlasting joy.

Although neither in life nor death have the heirs yet obtained their inheritance, yet it is guaranteed to them in a testament which "cannot be broken"; for its divine Executor is able to carry out all its provisions even though it require the raising of most of the heirs from the dead. Christ is related to that will as Testator, Executor, Surety, and Heir. In human affairs these offices would require four different persons, but when they all center in Christ they have an illustrative use which must not be strained beyond that point which they are intended to elucidate. Thus the words Lamb, Lion, Vine, Door, Sacrifice, High Priest, Advocate, Judge, &c., do not conflict at all as applied to Christ, but are only used to describe the various attributes displayed by Him in so many parts and portions of His work. For instance, His first coming to suffer was like a "Lamb"; His future coming to conquer will be as a "Lion."—Isa. liii, 7: John i, 29: Rev. v, 5.

3. By what means will the inheritance be obtained? In the present state men are disqualified from holding everlasting or eternal possession of their property on account of *death*, and death itself is the result of *sin*—" By one man's disobedience sin entered into the world, and death by sin."—Rom. v, 12. How then can we get rid of sin and death? Divine mercy has provided a way for us. " Christ died for our sins."—1 Cor. xv, 3. " God so loved the world, that He gave His only begotten Son, that whosoever believeth in Him should not perish, but have *everlasting* life." John iii, 16. It is therefore " by means of " the death of Christ that the inheritance is made possible. This enables us to understand why His blood is called " the blood of the everlasting covenant," or the " blood of the *new testament* shed for many for the *remission of sins*."—Heb. xiii, 20: Mat. xxvi, 28. Hence learn the preciousness of that inheritance, from the fact that Christ has died to secure it for us. And so the whole blood-washed throng of heirs—those who lived before as well as those who lived after His death—will meet in the resurrection and unite with grateful hearts and voices in the song of redemption, saying, " Thou wast slain and hast redeemed us to God *by thy blood* out of every kindred, and tongue, and people, and nation,

and hast made us unto our God kings and priests; and we shall reign *on the earth.*"—Rev. 5, 10.

See that glorified inheritance of the saints in light! a perpetual paradise restored! populous with bright forms! resounding with angelic odes! and teeming with all pleasant things! And when you contemplate these things remember the agony and the tears which the holy Saviour endured to purchase them for you. And now He promises that if you will do His commandments, He will give you a right—even a *right*—to the tree of life. Oh what condescending love! that a sinner without a right even to a crumb of bread or breath of air, should be offered a *right* to the tree of life in the midst of the paradise of God! The Saviour's enriching love is free to the humblest, and mighty to save. Take an instance from His walks among men. On some of the uplands leading from the great and fertile plain of Esdraelon, stood the little city of Nain reposing in the quiet sunlight amid the verdant fields and vineyards of that favored land. But sadness reigns in at least one household of that city, for lo! a funeral train is winding like a wintry shadow along the streets and issuing forth from one of the gates. The corpse is borne by sympathizing friends; it is a *young* man, cut down in the morning of his days, torn from the cheerful society of young persons before the plans of his life had even begun to be realized perhaps. This was a startling stroke, but what makes it still more distressing, he was "the *only* son of his mother," and, sadder still, "*she a widow.*" In that vast procession—for there was much people of the city with her—I can almost imagine that I can see her tottering along, almost blinded with swift-falling tears; her head bowed with woe, and her heart *almost* broken as she thinks "who will care for mother now?" But ah! just over the hills another company is approaching to meet them by the same pathway. The blessed Jesus, the great Prophet of Israel, is there, and His disciples, and throngs of people with Him. And little does the weeping mother know whose all-seeing and pitying eye has already "had compassion on her." The gentle Saviour has comprehended the whole scene at a glance, and says unto her "Weep not." Then He came and touched the coffin, and they that bare him stood still. As if His gentle heart was too full for words, He makes that speaking gesture with His hand, "Stop!" And what a blest obedience was that! Suppose they had gone on; His own mother could have advised them, "Whatsoever *He* saith unto you, do:"—a golden saying which all of us ought to let "sink down into" our hearts, and echo its musical sweetness along the vista of our pilgrimage, through all the scenes of life. "Whatsoever *He* saith unto you do," for there is a blessing in it. Well, they stood still. And now a solemn hush comes over that vast assembly, with one thrilling moment of suspense, when probably not a sound was heard but the too uncontrollable sobbings of the mother; and there sounds out on the air the sweet and heavenly voice of Jesus, "young man I say unto thee arise;"—"And he that was dead sat up and began to speak," and "He delivered him to his mother." After rescuing him from the bloody jaws of the grave-worm, the Saviour might have claimed him for His attendant or body-servant, as it were; but no, He gave him back to his mother. There was much for that young man to do in his own humble sphere. "Let every little candle shine, you in your corner and I in mine." Perhaps the young man was needful to the comfort of his widowed mother, and the Saviour would thus teach all young persons "to show piety at home, and to *requite* their parents: for this is *good and acceptable* before God."--1 Tim. v, 4. The Saviour himself even in the rack of agony which we suffered on the cross did not forget to make provision for His mother, by commending her to the care of the beloved disciple. This great miracle teaches that the Saviour watches over the needs of parents, and pities their bereavements. "The eyes of the Lord are in every place beholding the evil and the good." Fathers and mothers, who then can be so dear to you as the Lord Jesus? I beseech you to come to Jesus yourselves and bring your children with you. "The Lord said unto Noah come thou and all thy house into the ark."

Oh that we had some Andrews here. He had a way of bringing his friends to Jesus. He brought Peter that afterwards became such a great apostle. On another occasion some Greeks desired to see Jesus and there we find Andrew again lending his assistance. But is there one in this house to-day who says, "No one cares for *me?*" Let poor old blind Bartimeus tell you that you are mistaken. As he sat by the wayside begging he heard a commotion of many voices and footsteps and when he enquired what it was they told him "Jesus of Nazareth passeth by." No doubt he had heard of the Saviour's great miracles, and so he cried out, "Jesus thou Son of David, have mercy on me." But the persons around him told him to "hold his peace." Not discouraged by their coldness however, he cried the more, "Son of David, have mercy on me." And though every body seemed to scorn him, no one to take him by the hand or give him one word of encouragement, yet the blessed Saviour's own quick ear had heard that humble cry, and so He stood still and commanded the poor blind man to be called unto Him. Then see how quickly the popular voice is changed; they had rebuked him before, but now they say "Be of good comfort, rise; *He* calleth thee." And so he came and was healed and followed Jesus.—Mar. x, 46-52. So then, whether any one else invites you or not, "be of good comfort, rise; *He* calleth thee."

SIXTH DISCOURSE.

IMMORTALITY, AND HOW IT MAY BE OBTAINED.

"God so loved the world that He gave His only begotten Son, that whosoever believeth in Him should not perish but have everlasting life."—JNO. III, 16.

The word immortality means "never-dying existence." It therefore, of course, implies the idea of eternal or everlasting life, Correct views on this question are very necessary to a clear understanding and full appreciation of the gospel of the kingdom. It is thought by some that every person, however wicked, is already in possession of immortality. But according to Cruden's Concordance the word immortality occurs but five times in the Bible (Apocrypha always excepted), and is never applied to sinners. *Once* we are told that Christ has brought it to light through the gospel. 2 Tim. i, 10. *Once* that *God only* hath it.—1 Tim. vi, 17. *Once* that we must "*seek for*" it. (Do you seek for what you already have?)—Rom. ii, 7. *Twice* that the righteous will put it on at *the resurrection.*—1 Cor. xv, 53, 54. Thus the immortality which the gospel offers to men is an *endless life manifested through an incorruptible body at the resurrection.* This immortality was exemplified or brought to light by the literal and bodily resurrection of Christ from the dead, to die no more: which resurrection is a precedent of ours—"Christ the firstfruits; afterward they that are Christ's at His coming."—1 Cor. xv, 23.*

The word "soul" is found several hundred times in the Bible, but the phrase "*immortal* soul" is never once used in that Holy Book. According to Cruden's Concordance, the word "immortal" occurs but *once* in the Bible, and is then applied not to the human soul but to *God*—"the King eternal, immortal, invisible."—1 Tim. i, 17. Having now shown that the phrases "immortal soul" and "immortality of the soul" (the pet phrases of some writers and speakers) are never found in the Bible, it follows that if mankind would observe the same silence as the Bible does concerning them we would never hear them used in human language. And surely "the law of the Lord is perfect, converting the soul," (Psa. xix, 7), and hence the whole gospel and the whole plan of redemption can be fully and effectually advocated without those phrases. The Bible contains enough words to express its own doctrines, and we should esteem it a virtue to expurgate from our faith such phrases as are neither found in nor justified by that Holy Book. How

---

* "Immortality, in the sacred writings, is never applied to the spirit of man. It is not the doctrine of Plato which the resurrection of Jesus proves. It is the *immortality of the body* of which his resurrection is a proof and pledge. This was never developed till He became the firstborn from the dead."
—A. CAMPBELL, in *"Christian System,"* p. 281, A.D. 1839.

then were these phrases brought into use? Chambers' Encyclopedia says, "The Egyptian nation appears to have been the first to declare that the soul was immortal."—Edition of 1876. But if it had been a doctrine of God, and of such importance as some think, we should suppose that *Israel* would have been the *first* to declare it, and not the abominable Egyptians; for "the secret of the Lord is with them that *fear* Him," and "the *meek* will He guide in judgment."—Psa. xxv, 9, 14. The Commentary of Jamieson, Faussett and Brown, highly extolled by preachers and college professors of various denominations, says, "No where is the immortality of the *soul*, distinct from the body taught: a notion which many erroneously have derived from heathen philosophers. Scripture does not contemplate the anomalous state brought about by death as the consummation to be earnestly looked for (2 Cor. v, 4), but the *resurrection*."—On 1 Cor. xv, 53. Some of the heathen philosophized not only on the conscious existence of the soul after leaving the body, but also before coming into it. Perhaps they thought the soul could get along as well without the body *before* inhabiting it as afterwards. But facts proved that men had no *recollection* of having lived in a previous life, and this objection threatened to explode the theory: with fertile invention however they affirmed that their souls, before coming into their present bodies, had to drink a cup of forgetfulness. But an early

Christian writer answered, "How then did they remember that cup?" And thus the tangled web of heathen philosophy on that point was proved to be "foolishness."

A reliable Greek and Hebrew scholar will testify that the words translated "soul" (*nephesh* in Hebrew and *psuche* in Greek) are in Genesis four times applied to fishes, fowls, and creeping things of the earth *before* they are applied to man. The English reader may see two of these instances by the marginal reading of Gen. i, 20, 30. And when applied to man in ch. ii, 7, it is not even then said that he became an immortal or *ever-living* soul, or that he had such a soul put into him; but simply, "man became a living soul." On this passage the American Bible Union says, "The Hebrew word (*nephesh*) here rendered *soul*, includes *all* beings that have animal life; and hence it is applied to animals of the sea and land in Gen. i, 20, 21, 24, 30. The English word *soul* (like the German *seele*) originally had this extent of meaning, as in verses 20, 30, in the margin of the common English version."—Genesis with Notes, 1873. These are stubborn and valuable facts which the sincere enquirer after *truth* will not dare to ignore. Do you not see then what a monstrous thing it would be to say that a soul is an *immortal* something which can live and act with an individuality of its own while the body is mouldering in the dust? Can any one suppose that every fish, fowl, &c., has an immortal part of that kind when he reads, "Let the waters bring forth abundantly the moving creature that hath *life* (margin *soul*)?"—Gen. i, 20. Would it not be profane to take a title which, occurring but once in Scripture, is applied to *God*, and apply that sacred title to every fish, fowl, and wicked man? When the Bible declares that "God ONLY hath immortality," would it not be a positive falsehood to say that every fish, fowl, and every man, however vile, has it also? Could we persistently affirm such a falsehood and hope to escape the lake of fire?—Rev. xxi, 8.

The "Speaker's Commentary," by "Bishops and other clergy of the Church of England," says on Gen. ii, 7, "*All* animals have the body, *all* the living *soul*, but the breath of life breathed into his nostrils by God himself is said of man alone." But neither does the phrase "breath of life" prove a present immortality in man for the lower animals *also* have the breath of life—" there went in unto Noah into the ark, two and two of all flesh wherein is the breath of life."—Gen. vii, 15, 22. "They have all *one* breath."—Eccles. iii, 19. What then is the true condition of the dead between death and the resurrection? Let the Bible answer. "The dead know not *anything*. . . There is no *work*, nor *device*, nor *knowledge*, nor *wisdom* in the *grave* (*hades*) whither thou goest." This proves them *unconscious* and *inactive;* and hence without either pleasure or pain. It is the night "when *no* man can work."—Jno. ix, 4; Eccl. ix, 5. "In that very day his *thoughts* perish."—Psa. cxlvi, 4. "His sons come to honour, and he *knoweth it not;* and they are brought low, but he *perceiveth it not* of them."—Job xiv, 21. "Thou art our Father, though Abraham be *ignorant* of us."—Isa. lxiii, 16. They "*dwell* in dust."—Isa. xxvi, 19. They "*sleep* in the dust of the earth." Dan. xii, 2. They "*sleep* in Jesus."—Jno. xi, 11, 14; 1 Thes. iv, 14. They have "not ascended into the heavens."—Ac. ii, 34. "I shall go to him" (2 Sam. xii, 23), means "I will go down into *the grave* unto my son."—Gen. xxxvii, 35. It is plain from these testimonies that the future reward of the righteous depends on the *resurrection*—they are to be recompensed "at the resurrection of the just," not at the death of the just.—Lu. xiv, 14. Paul, after naming some of his sufferings, makes all his hopes of compensation depend on the resurrection, saying, "What advantageth it me the dead *rise not?*'—1 Cor. xv, 32.* He did not preach Jesus and the immortal

---

* "What the apostle says here is a regular and legitimate conclusion from the doctrine, that *there is no resurrection;* for if there be no resurrection, then there can be no *judgment;* no future state of *rewards and punishments;* why, therefore, should we bear crosses and keep ourselves under continual discipline! Let us eat and drink, take all the pleasure we can, for to-morrow we die: and there is an end of us forever." —Adam Clarke. On Heb. xi, 19, the same writer says, "The

soul, as many now try to do, but "Jesus and the resurrection."—Ac. xvii, 18. With much force Adam Clarke says concerning the resurrection, "There is not a doctrine in the gospel on which more *stress* is laid; and there is not a doctrine in the present system of preaching which is treated with more *neglect.*" It is the theory of going to glory at death which causes the doctrine of the resurrection to be treated with so much neglect.* The personal coming of Christ, on which the resurrection depends, is also neglected from the same cause. In perfect and beautiful harmony with its teaching that the resurrection is the time of reward, the Bible also teaches that the second coming of Christ is the time of reward; so the two classes of testimony ought to be viewed together, one serving to strengthen and confirm the

resurrection of the dead must have been a doctrine of the patriarchs: they expected a heavenly inheritance; they saw they died as did other men; and they must have known that they could not enjoy it but in consequence of a *resurrection from the dead.*"

---

* "In putting souls in heaven, hell, and purgatory, ye *destroy* the arguments wherewith Christ and Paul prove the resurrection... If the souls be in heaven, tell me why they be not in as good case as the angels be? And then what cause is there of the resurrection?"–Tyndale, a great reformer and martyr of the sixteenth century—of whom Edwards' Encyclopedia says: "'To this great man we are under great obligations for our emancipation from the fetters of Popery."

other. We can have no resurrection before Christ comes, for "the Lord *himself* shall descend from heaven . . . and the dead in Christ shall rise."— 1 Thes. iv, 16. And "*then* shall He reward every man according to his work."—Mat. xvi, 27. "When the chief Shepherd shall appear ye shall receive a crown of glory that fadeth not away."—1 Pet. v, 4. "It is a righteous thing with God to recompense affliction to those who afflict you, and to you who are afflicted rest with us, *at the revelation of the Lord Jesus.*" A. B. Union's translation of 2 Thes. i, 6, 7. Here we perceive that neither the "affliction" (*thlipsis*) pertaining to the wicked, nor the "rest" (*anesis*) pertaining to the righteous will be received before He comes. It is a mistake to suppose, as some have done, that the word "rest" in the last quotation is a *verb*; for it is as much a *noun* as the word "tribulation" or "affliction" in the same quotation. Paul is here teaching that the Lord, at His coming, will recompense two things—to the one party "affliction;" to the other "rest." And "let us labor therefore to enter into *that* rest." Heb. iv, 11. From Paul we learn that the advent and resurrection will occur under "the *last* trumpet," and from John that the *seventh* is the last (for he makes no mention of an eighth), also that under it the kingdom of God will be established on earth, and the "reward given to small and great."—1 Thes. iv, 16; 1 Cor. xv, 52; with Rev.

xi, 15-18. Till He come, therefore, the righteous dead must calmly sleep in the revolving earth as if rocked in some great cradle and hymned over by the zephyr and the storm. Have you not seen a loving mother go to her child and, thinking it had slept long enough, gently place her hand upon its brow and wake it up? Well, "precious in the eyes of the Lord is the death of His saints." He marks the moments of their slumbers, and will send a beautiful white-robed angel by-and-by to awaken each of them and say, perhaps in the very words of Scripture, "The Master is come and calleth for thee."

Having now proved that man in the present state does not possess immortality, and having traced out his whereabouts from the morning of creation to the morning of the resurrection, let us next enquire what will become of him *at* the resurrection? If righteous he will enter upon the enjoyment of the promised inheritance and of all the shining rewards of a blissful eternity. He will be qualified for those eternal joys by the gift of that immortality or eternal life which is obtained not by nature, but through Christ alone; for "the wages of sin is death, but the gift of God is eternal life *through our Lord Jesus Christ*."—Rom. vi, 23. But when the wicked stand before Him who "was ordained of God to be the Judge of quick and dead," they will be sentenced to "everlasting destruction from the presence of the Lord and from the glory of His power."—Ac. 10, 42: 2 Thes. i, 9. There is a great abundance of testimony to prove the grand truth that, after being condemned at the judgment, the wicked shall be blotted out of existence; but surely the following selections ought to be enough to convince all who are not blinded by sheer prejudice:—"The day cometh that shall burn as an oven, and all the proud, yea and all that do wickedly, shall be stubble; and the day that cometh shall *burn them up*, saith the Lord of Hosts, that it shall leave them neither *root nor branch*. . . And ye shall tread down the wicked, for they shall be ASHES under the soles of your feet in the day that I shall do this, *saith the Lord of Hosts*."—Mal. iv, 1, 3. "The enemies of the Lord shall be as the *fat of lambs;* they shall *consume;* into smoke shall they *consume away* . . Yet a little while and the wicked shall *not be*."—Psa. xxxvii, 10, 20. "The wicked shall be *silent* in darkness."—1 Sam. ii, 9. They shall be " no more."—Psa. civ, 35. They shall be "as nothing."—Isa. xli, 12: Jer. x, 24. They shall pass away and perish " as a snail which melteth," and " as wax melteth before the fire."—Psa. lviii, 8; lxviii, 2. " They shall be utterly burned with fire."—2 Sam. xxiii, 6, 7. They shall be burned up as *chaff* or *tares* of the field.—Mat. iii, 12: xiii, 30, 40. To express their doom in a sentence, " They shall be *as though they had not been*."— Obadiah 16. Could any human ingenuity frame words into sentences that would more clearly and completely express the utter and final extinction of the wicked? After sinning, Adam was driven out of Eden lest he should eat of the tree of life and live *forever*. An immortal sinner would be a calamity in the universe. *

Death is the severest penalty known to human law. It is called "capital *punishment*," and if never relieved or broken up by a resurrection, would it not be an *everlasting* punishment? Now the Bible does not say "the wages of sin is *torture*," but "the wages of sin is *death*."—Rom. vi, 23. And that will be the "everlasting punishment" threatened against the wicked, "the second death," a death from which there will be no awakening. Scripture clearly explains what is meant by "the fire that shall not be quenched"; for in Jer. xvii, 27, we read, "I will kindle a fire in the gates thereof, and it shall devour the palaces of Jerusalem, and it shall not be quenched." The fulfillment of this prediction is recorded in Jer. lii, 13: Lam. iv, 11. Of course that fire is not

---

* "He drove him out of paradise, and removed him from the tree of life because He pitied him, (and did not desire) that he should continue a sinner forever, nor that the sin which surrounded him should be immortal, and evil interminable."—Irenaeus (about A.D. 175) B. iii. c. xxiii. "Gregory Nazianzen (born about 328) says the exclusion from the tree of life was that evil might not be immortal, and that punishment might be an act of benevolence."—*Speaker's Commentary*.

burning now. When we say that a fire in a burning house could not be quenched, we mean simply that it *consumed* the house, don't we? Eusebius, a learned Greek ecclesiastical historian, relates (B. vi, c. 41) that "Epimachus and Alexander, who had continued for a long time in prison, enduring innumerable sufferings from scourges and scrapers, were also destroyed in *puri asbesto*"— the very same words which in Mat. iii, 12, and Lu. iii, 17, are translated "unquenchable fire." Must we suppose the fire which consumed those two martyrs to be burning yet, simply because it is called unquenchable? Notice that the fire shall burn "the carcasses" of the wicked, and that a carcass is neither a disembodied soul nor a *living* body; but, according to Webster, "a *dead* body of an animal, decaying remains of an animal." It is therefore the *body* which will be cast into that fire. Isa. lxvi, 24: Mat. v, 29, 30. When the carcasses of various animals were burned as the offal of ancient cities, the worms would consume what the fire did not. Neither the worms nor fire *preserved* those carcasses. We read of "everlasting fire," or, which is the same, "eternal fire," called so because its *effects* or *results* will be eternal, just as the "eternal redemption" and "eternal judgment" will be eternal in their effects or results, not that the acts of redeeming and judging will be always going on.—Heb. vi, 2, and ix, 12. The effect of the everlasting or eternal fire will be to reduce the wicked to *ashes*, for that was its effect in former times—" turning the cities of Sodom and Gomorrha into *ashes*." Compare Jude 7 with 2 Pet. ii, 6. If allowed to theorize, I would say that perhaps it will be an *electric* fire, like ten thousand thunderbolts focalized, for the occasion, into a very "lake of fire." And who can say that electricity, even in its invisible or diffused state, is not an "eternal" element of the material universe?

Many who advocate endless torture tell us that the fire will not be *literal;* pangs of conscience being the real torment. I think this notion started about A.D. 200, with Origen, of whom Adam Clarke says that he was " capable of believing and teaching the most absurd notions for grave truths." Would not this be almost neutralizing future punishment, especially in the case of those who deserve it most, namely, those who have become so steeped in sin as to be already "*past* feeling," "having their conscience seared as with a hot iron."—1 Tim. iv, 2; Ephes. iv, 19. Surely the advocates of that theory would not dare to *allegorize* the *history* of Sodom and Gomorrha as they do the *prophecy* of of the future fire! The *literal* burning of the wicked in those two cities has been "set forth for an *example*" of the future punishment.—Jude 7; Lu. 17, 26, 29. It was a *literal* fire which consumed the sacrifice and the armed men.—1 Kin. 18, 38; 2 Kin. i, 10-14. Surely then "Upon the wicked

He shall reign snares," (margin, " Or, *quick burning coals*") fire and brimstone, and an horrible tempest (margin, "Or, *a burning tempest*"): this shall be the portion of their cup.—Psalms xi, 6. The vague notion just referred to concerning the *nature* of future punishment reminds me of an equally vague and mystifying notion concerning the *place* of it. A prominent preacher of the Methodist denomination said (according to a newspaper report of his discourse) that he did not know whether hell is "above or below." I would like to ask him if he ever heard of such a thing as going *up* to hell? When we read concerning a certain class of sinners that "the smoke of their torment ascendeth up forever," we must remember that even in the legal precision of the law of Moses "forever" has a *limited* meaning—"he shall serve him *forever*," that is, until the *death* of the servant or master, for in death the servant is free from his master.—Job iii, 19; Ex. xxi, 6. The "forever" in Jonah 2, 6, lasted only three days and nights. But Im not saying that "forever" has *everywhere* a limited meaning, for it is a sound rule concerning the Greek *aiōn*, translated "forever," that, as the *Enc. Rel. Knowl.* says, "It must always be taken in the sense of *unlimited* duration, unless something appears in the subject or connection in which it occurs to *limit* its signification." Now, when applied to the conscious torment which the wicked will endure before expiring, something *does* appear in such a subject or connection, to *limit* its signification, for I have heaped up testimony which abundantly proves the wicked to be of a perishable and mortal nature. ☞ It is a fact of deep significance that they are not compared to anything fire-proof or indestructible, but only to the most evanescent and cumbustible materials, as CHAFF, STUBBLE, TARES, FAT OF LAMBS, &c. Throughout the Bible we are taught "the wages of sin is DEATH" (Rom. vi, 23); but it was the Serpent, the father of lies, who first denied this great truth, and, with as much bombast and solemnity as if he had been delivering a modern oration against it, said, "Ye shall *not* surely *die,* for God doth know that in the day ye eat thereof, then your eyes shall be opened, and ye shall be as gods, knowing good and evil."—Jno. viii, 44; Gen. iii, 4, 5. This bears a startling resemblence to the assertion of many who are still affirming sinners to be immortal and capable of existing and sinning as long as God and the angels live—in endless duration. But it is a libel on our poor mortal race to say we are capable of perpetrating an eternity of crime. With all our faults we are not so bad as that, for if, in the day of the Lord, we shall not be found worthy of endless life in holiness and happiness we shall not obtain endless life of any kind, but will only obtain "the wages of sin."*

---

* "Many of the primitive fathers in the church explicitly

The following passages explain one another: "Then shall the dust return to the earth as it was; and the *spirit* (*pneuma*) shall return to God who gave it."—Eccles. xii, 7. "His *breath* (*pneuma*) goeth forth, he returneth to his earth."—Psa. cxlvi, 4. "Thou takest away their *breath* (*pneuma*), they die, and return to their dust."—Psa. civ, 29. "The body without the *spirit* (*pneuma*; margin, *breath*) is dead."—Jas. ii, 26. In the Greek it is the same word, *pneuma*, here translated "breath" and "spirit." The first passage affirms that God gave the spirit or breath which returns, for it is *He* that "giveth to all life and *breath*;" it was *He* that breathed into man the *breath* of life.—Ac. xvii, 26; Gen. ii, 7. The second passage, being added to the first, affirms that although the spirit or breath returneth to God yet THE MAN HIMSELF, as indicated by the masculine personal pronoun "*he*, returned to his earth," and so they separate. Why should you be surprised that the man proper, the real person, the man himself, goes to dust? has not the divine sentence postively *required* this?—"Unto dust shalt *thou* return."—

---

maintained the natural *mortality* of the soul."—*Baptist Library*, 1846, vol. 1, p. 485. "I think we are not warranted in concluding (as some have done) so positively concerning this question as to make it a point of Christian faith to interpret figuratively and not literally the 'death' and 'destruction' spoken of in Scripture as the doom of the condemned; and to insist on the belief that they are kept alive *forever*."—Archbishop WHATELY, *Future State*, p. 185.

Gen. iii, 19. Would the return of the mere *body* to the dust, while the personal "he" or "thou" escapes to immediate glory be a fulfillment of this law? If you believe Solomon when he says "the spirit shall return to God" you are equally bound to believe him when he says, "the dead know not anything," and that, as to the item of death, both man and beast "go unto *one* place."—Eccles. iii, 20; ix, 5. But this is no denial of future rewards and punishments, for he also affirms that "God shall bring every work into judgment," which implies man's *resurrection.*—Eccles. xii, 14.

In the promise to the thief Griesbach notices a Greek reading which has no comma between "thee" and "to-day." Placing the comma after "to-day," I would understand the promise to mean, I say unto thee *to-day*, that is, I promptly give thee a *present* assurance as a comfort in a dying hour, that thou shalt be with me in the paradise at my coming. The word "to-day" might also be a precious reminder to the supplicant that in his particular case the prayer was not too late, but came "*while* it is called to-day."—Heb. iii, 13. It is not only our right but our *duty* to alter the punctuation when the sense requires it, for the punctuation of the Bible, either in Greek or English, was not placed there by the *inspired* writers, but is a human invention.* I may remark that

---

* "The sacred writings had originally, and for a long time,

"shalt thou be," in the Saviour's answer, was not intended by the old English translation as a question, any more than "unto dust shalt thou return," in Gen. iii, 19. The A. B. U. translation reads "thou shalt be," which agrees better with the usage of modern English. Notice the inconsistency of those who tell you that the pronoun "thou" in the promise to the thief means his immortal soul, but that the same "thou" in the sentence "unto dust shalt *thou* return" means only the mortal body. *Sēmeron* ("to-day") is an adverb occurring in the New Testament thirty-nine times, and is rendered "to-day" eighteen times, and "this day" twenty-one times. In the single book of Deut., I find seven occurrences of *s¯meron* having the comma *after* it, both in the Greek and English version.—Deut. iv, 40; xi, 8, 13, 28; xiii, 18; xix, 9; xxviii, 1; also Ac. xxvi, 29. For another instance of declaring to-day, something to be done at a future time, see

no *punctuation*, nor any such divisions as those of *chapter* and *verse*. The words were not so much as separated by intervals from one another. So late even as the *fifth* century the New Testament had none of the ordinary marks. They form as the reader has seen, no part of the original text, but are mere *human* contrivances. The punctuation is *often* very *faulty*. In some of the early printed editions the points seem to have been put in almost at random, and even in the *present* Greek text, as well as in the *English* version the sense and beauty of many passages are marred by injudicious and inaccurate punctuation."—*Comprehensive Commentary*, vol. 6.

Zech. ix, 12, 13. Three days afterwards the blessed Saviour said that He had "*not yet ascended*" to His Father; how then can you suppose that the penitent thief went there with Him on the very day of the crucifixion? It sounds inconsistent when we hear people say that the holy apostles were required to wait until a place should be "*prepared*," and the Saviour "come again" to them, but that the penitent thief did not have to wait at all but went there immediately to death. To understand the answer of the Lord, you must understand the prayer of the thief—he did not say, "Lord remember me when thou *goest*," but "when thou *comest* in thy kingdom," referring to the second coming when the kingdom will be established on earth. As Archbishop Whately has said, "*Into* thy kingdom is a mistranslation; it should be 'in thy kingdom.' The meaning is 'at thy *second coming*' in triumphant glory."—Future State, p. 250. It is the same kind of expression as "when the Son of man cometh *in* His glory."—Mat. xxv, 31. In both places the Greek is not *eis* (*into*), but *en* (*in*). The American Bible Union has therefore given the correct translation, "Lord remember me when thou comest *in* thy kingdom." The answer agrees with this,—"Thou shalt be with me in *the paradise* (*tō paradeiso*)"; for the kingdom will be a blissful restored paradise on earth. Liddell and Scott define *pradeisos* (i. e. paradise), to be "a park, or pleasure-grounds;

an oriental word used by the LXX for the *garden of Eden.*" The Greek version of Gen. ii, 8, 9, 10, 16, and iii, 3, 23, has paradeisos where the English has "*garden.*" And that paradise which once existed on earth will be permanently restored to the redeemed in a larger and infinitely better form when the now groaning and inanimate creation shall participate with them in "the glorious liberty of the children of God."—Rom. viii, 21; Isa. li, 3, and xi, 9; Num. xiv, 21; Rev. ii, 7, and xxi, 5. But Paul seems to speak of paradise and a third heaven as the same, why then does he say "caught *up* into paradise," if it is to be on earth? It may be spoken of as "up" because though on earth it will be a higher or more exalted state of existence than the persecuted and suffering life he was then leading. But this phrase contains no "up" in the Greek. Campbell's version (1832) renders it, "snatched away into paradise," and "snatched away to the third heaven." In both places it is *arpazo* that is rendered "snatched away"; and in three Lexicons I do not find to "catch *up*" among its meanings. In Ac. viii, 39, it is properly rendered "caught away," and in John vi, 15, "take by force." Paul's words accurately translated would be "snatched away to *a* third heaven," "snatched away into *the* paradise." Peter speaks of three heavens as consecutively pertaining to earth—(1) those which "were of old;" (2) those "which are now;" and (3) the future or "new heavens and earth wherein dwelleth righteousness."—2 Peter iii, 5, 7, 13. And that future heaven, when fully revealed, especially in the endless bliss beyond the Millennium, will be "a *third* heaven" or "the paradise" restored and far eclipsing the lost paradise. I suppose Paul meant that he had been favored prophetically with transporting and rapturous "visions and revelations" (ver. 1) of that future paradise, which it was not yet allowable to utter; somewhat as John was told to "seal up" what the seven thunders uttered.—Rev. x, 4. And that as to the manner of receiving them, he did not know whether those visions were communicated to him corporeally, or, as John says, "in the spirit." Rev. xxi, 10.

When he says, "Whilst we are at home in the body we are absent from the Lord," he does not mean that if in the *resurrection* body he would be absent from the Lord, for he declares that to be the very time when we shall be "ever with the Lord."—1 Thes. iv, 16. He was willing to be "absent from the body," but not by being "unclothed" (for he, and Hezekiah before him, had already objected to *that*), but rather by being "clothed upon" by that eternal house—the resurrection body—and in *that* way be absent from "this *vile* body." This is not the *disembodied* absence of which Plato and Socrates philosophized, and of which a certain class of moderns profess to be so desirous.—2 Cor. v, 4, 8 : Isa. xxxviii, 11, 14. Paul clearly indicated that he did not desire to be unclothed, and we should not so misconstrue his "desire to depart and be with Christ" as to make him contradict himself. This verb "to depart" is *analuo* (whence came the English "analyze"), and in Lu. xii, 36, is translated "*return*." But in Phil. i, 23, it is the infinitive with the article, and the celebrated Greek grammar of Kuhner says, "The infinitive with the article is treated in all respects like a *substantive*." Why then might we not understand Paul as here expressing his desire for the *return* of Christ? But the words are plain enough as they stand, when we remember that the dead are *asleep* and they "know not anything"; hence, as they cannot count the flight of years, the moment of death seems to them to be the moment of being with Christ, in the resurrection morning; as though on a bed of pain, with weeping friends around them, they had closed their eyes for an imperceptible moment, and suddenly, with a start and a thrill awoke to the glories of the resurrection morning to find the great Redeemer here, and bright angels crowding into the room.

There is no mystery about the souls under the altar (Rev. vi, 9,) when you remember that the death of a martyr was compared to offering a sacrifice on an altar. Thus Paul says, "Even if I am *poured out* on the *sacrifice* and ministration of your faith, I rejoice."—A. B. U. version of Phil. ii, 17. And when about to be put to death by Nero, he said, "I am now ready to be offered."— 2 Tim, iv, 6. Concerning the aged Polycarp who suffered martyrdom about A.D. 160, his biographer says, that "Placing his hands behind him, and being bound like a distinguished ram out of a great flock for sacrifice, and prepared to be an acceptable burnt offering unto God," he gave thanks and prayed that he might be an "*acceptable sacrifice.*" The ancient *literal* altar of burnt offering was made "hollow with boards," overlaid with brass, hence called the brazen altar. When the *flesh* of the sacrifice was offered on this altar the blood was poured out "at the bottom" of it.—Ex. xxvii, 8; Lev. iv, 30. Hence, the blood when thus poured out and saturating the earth, would be "under the altar."* And notice particularly that the Greek version of Lev. xvii, 14, says, "The *life* (Greek *psuche, soul*) of all flesh is the blood thereof"—*psuche pasēs sarkos haima autou esti.* We may therefore, by metonomy, speak of the blood of the martyr under the altar, as the *soul* of the martyr crying "How long?" Thus Abel's blood cried from the ground unto God, and if that cry had been hieroglyphically represented,

---

* "The altar is upon earth, not in heaven."—ADAM CLARKE. "Under the altar of God, that is under the earth."—VICTORINUS, towards the close of the third century.

as under the fifth seal, it might have been described as the voice of the blood of Abel crying out and saying, "How long, O Lord, dost thou not avenge my blood upon Cain?" The "white robes" were appointed to them by divine *decree*, just as in the present tense it is said, "All things *are* yours."—1 Cor. iii, 22.

Whether the discourse concerning the rich man and Lazarus (Lu. xvi) be a parable, or whether it be a prophecy containing some parabolic expressions, it would be contrary to common sense and the sound rules of interpretation to make it conflict with the undoubtedly plain and literal testimonies of Scripture. It is well agreed that we must always interpret the figurative by the literal and so as to harmonize with the literal. It would never do to reverse this rule. Hence after reading so many literal testimonies that the dead are unconscious till the resurrection, we may not expect the rich man and Lazarus to teach anything to the contrary. To turn every word of this discourse into a *literal history* of a disembodied state would require the literal Moses and the literal prophets, all in a disembodied state; and the "five brethren," though still in the body, would have to hear those instructors personally, instead of hearing their *writings*. And, as some one has said, what a vast "bosom" too Abraham would have, to *literally* hold all the righteous who have died since his time! The discourse therefore contains *figures* of speech, as all must admit. It does not once mention "soul" or "spirit," but points to *bodily* existence, as the eyes, finger, water, tongue, and flame indicate.* The reason given why there could be no passing between the two places indicates the same— "between us and you there is a great *gulf* (Greek *chasma*) fixed." Would a gulf or *chasm* be any obstacle to an immaterial and disembodied soul? And is it to be supposed that such souls in heaven and hell do literally see and converse with one another, the one class begging for mercy, and the other refusing it? for "*you*" (*humōn*) is as truly plural here as "us," which indicates that the rich man was but one of a *class* or *company* spoken to. It might be thought a parable, in which, to show the importance of hearing Moses and the prophets, *lifeless* persons or things are *personified* after the example of the trees going forth to anoint a king (Judg. ix, 8); or Abel's blood crying from the ground (Gen. iv, 10); or the stone crying out of the wall, and the beam of the timber answering it (Hab. ii, 11); or Rachel weeping for her children, and refusing to be comforted.—Mat. ii, 18. † I call

---

* "The very circumstance of the torturing flames, implies, literally the presence of the *body;* and therefore cannot be literally true of a state in which the soul is *separate* from the body."—ARCHBISHOP WHATELY, *Future State*, p. 59.

† "She is *figuratively* represented as rising from her tomb and uttering a double lament for the loss of her children." —Commentary of Jamieson, Faussett and Brown.

7

the latter an instance of personification because if Rachel was unconscious in death she knew nothing of the massacre, but if alive in heaven she was beyond weeping and sorrow. In at least two of these personifications " holy men of God spake as they were moved by the *Holy Ghost.*"—2 Pet. i, 21. And the *Father* himself personifies the blood of Abel. Why then might not the *Son* use the same figure of speech with regard to the rich man and Lazarus? But I am inclined to view it as a *prophecy*, calling "those things which be not as though they were" (Rom. iv, 17), and pointing to Jewish affairs at the second advent of the Messiah. And of course those who first heard it did not know *how near* that advent might be, nor but what it might occur in their own life time. Nor do those Jews *now* living know but what it may occur in *their* lifetime. Ever since it was first spoken therefore it has been a warning to that people (whether they will heed it or not) on the importance of hearing Moses and the prophets. Three things cause me to think it relates to "*Israel* after the *flesh*: 1st, The rich man though in torment calls Abraham father, and Abraham calls him son; which seems to intimate only the *natural* relationship, for what other could be appropriate? I do not see why these terms of relationship should be used concerning an unconverted or apostate *Gentile*; 2d, There are five brethren, the Rich man making six—exactly the number of Abraham's sons by

Keturah, all "born after *the flesh*,"—Gen. xxv, 1, 2; 3d, No Scriptures are mentioned but "Moses and the prophets," the natural Israel refusing to hear the New Testament writers, even to this day.

About the time of the second advent there will be a considerable number of Jews in Palestine having "silver and gold, cattle and goods."—Eze. xxxviii, 8–13. These, I suppose, like the wealthy and covetous Pharisees of old, will claim the right to "sit in Moses' seat" (Mat. xxiii, 2,) and to domineer politically and ecclesiastically over "the poor of the flock," then present among them; for "the poor ye have always with you."—Zec. xi, 11; Deut. xv, 11; Mat. xxvi, 11. Now if the latter class be "Lazarus," the former would be "the rich man," one being put for a multitude; just as we now say "the rich man" or "the poor man," meaning two *classes* of men. Now remember that not all the Jews living at the time of Messiah's coming will be converted and saved, for there will be a rebellious class which the Lord will "purge out from among them."—Eze. xx, 38; Zec. xiii, 8. And of what class will the remnant be composed? I think we have the answer here, "I will also leave in the midst of thee an *afflicted* and *poor* people, and they shall trust in the name of the Lord."— Zeph. iii, 12. And this, it seems to me, identifies that spared remnant with the Lazarus of Lu. xvi. But why then is Lazarus said to die? My answer is that the verb "died" (*apothnēsko*), which is applied to him and the rich man, does not always imply a *literal* death; for, according to Greenfield, one of its meanings is, "to die to anything i. e. renounce, refuse submission to." The very same word is used by Paul to express his *conversion*—" For I through law *died* to law, that I might live to God."—Gal. ii, 19—American Bible Union's version. Why then might not the same word apply to the conversion of Paul's modern brethren (of which his own conversion seems to have been "a pattern"; 1 Tim. i, 16,) when, beholding Him " whom they have pierced," they shall welcome Him with shouts of " Blessed is He that cometh in the name of the Lord ?"—Mat. xxiii, 39. And being converted to the Messiah at His coming, and having thus "died" to the Mosaic law they will in this way be carried into terms of friendship with, or, as it were into " the bosom of Abraham," who, in a resurrected and immortal state, will then be dwelling on the land long ago covenanted to him. But "the rich man," what will become of his class? If this class be the rebellious portion of that nation, or " the fat and the strong," the Lord says, " I will *destroy* the fat and the strong, I will feed them with judgment."—Eze. xxxiv, 16. They will, in the first place, experience a political and ecclesiastical death in being deprived of place and power debarred from Messianic blessings, and driven to the place of their final destruction. Now if the prodigal son in the strange land was " dead " (Lu.

xv, 24), why might not these excommunicated and death-sentenced exiles be spoken of as both dead and buried? Then if while "tormented" in "the fiery indignation" that will soon reduce them to ashes, they lift up their eyes and "see Abraham in the kingdom of God" (Lu. xiii, 28), he will send no relief because there will be some impassable *chasm* between them and the Lazarus class; for the latter, though converted, will still be in the mortal body. But at this crisis I suppose the *ten* tribes will be still in their dispersion, for "the tents of *Judah*" are to be saved *first*.—Zec. xii, 7. If then the tormented class desire the Lazarus class to be sent off on a mission to those tribes—the balance of their "father's house"—the answer might be, "If they hear not Moses and the prophets, neither will they be persuaded, though one rose from the dead." The sin of the Jews was and is the not believing Moses and the prophets. The Saviour said, " Had ye believed Moses ye would have believed me, for he wrote of me."—Jno. v, 46.* A vail of blindness is upon their heart in

---

* Among many other proofs which ought to convince them of his being the true Messiah, and that He has *once* been on earth, may be named the following prophecies long ago fulfilled in him: He was to be born of a virgin—Gen. iii, 15; Isa. vii, 14;—Of the family of David—Psa. cxxxii, 11; Isa. xi, 1, and Jer. xxiii, 5;—In the town of Bethlehem—Mic. v, 2;—Was to suffer death by violent hands—Psa. xxii, 13-18;—Was to be buried—Isa. liii, 9;—But would rise again

reading Moses, but a time shall come when "the vail shall be taken away."—2 Cor. iii, 15, 16; Rom. xi, 7, 25. But why would the sending of the Lazarus class be as the sending of one "from the dead?" Because the conversion or "receiving" of them had been as "life from the dead."—Rom. xi, 15. And thus I have briefly sketched what seems to me a very probable interpretation of the rich man and Lazarus.

The mistaken idea that every man has innate and unconditional immortality is a foundation on which are built the following errors : 1, Metempsychosis, or the transmigration of souls into the bodies of beasts, birds or fishes. Edwards' Encyclopedia says this doctrine "prevails at the present day almost universally among the heathen nations of the *East;*" 2, Praying to the dead; 3, Purgatory; 4, Swedenborgianism; 5, The so-called "Spiritualism"; 6, Denial of the literal and bodily resurrection, affirming that the body is only a prison and that the soul can get along well enough without it; 7, Depreciating the importance of the

---

before seeing corruption—Psa. xvi, 10. And even the *time* in which He would appear and die, and the destruction of the city and temple that would follow, were specified; which time, "seventy weeks," i. e. 490 years in prophetic style, has *long since passed*, and the city and temple have long ago been destroyed.—Dan. ix, 24-26. But neither do they heed those prophets nor Moses himself, who warned them that if they would not hear the Messiah they would be destroyed.—Ac. iii, 22, 23.

second advent and the resurrection, and affirming
that we are rewarded at death, in a disembodied
state; 8, Depreciating the importance of the promised inheritance which the righteous will obtain in
the kingdom that God will establish *on earth;* and
affirming that as soon as they die they go to an
inheritance beyond the skies; 9, Depreciating the
merits of Christ through whom alone and by whose
death we can obtain everlasting life, and affirming that we obtained it through Adam and by our
natural birth; 10, Denial of a literal fire as the
instrument of future punishment. [I suppose this
is done because they cannot see how a material fire
could hurt an "immaterial soul"]; 11, Endless
existence in a state of torture and blasphemy. This
however has been found so thought-withering that
some have endeavored to soften it by advocating, 12,
The salvation of unconverted heathen idolaters; 13,
The salvation of every *sincere* errorist; 14, Universal salvation.

Briefly stated, the following is the *Scriptural*
doctrine concerning immortality, and it is a
misunderstanding of some texts which causes them
to be brought forward as if they conflicted with
those here quoted.

1. ☞ Immortality (i. e. eternal life) is not
inherited by nature, and at birth, but is to be
obtained only through Christ, and by none but the
righteous.☜   Proof: "The gift of God is eternal life *through* our Lord Jesus Christ."—Rom. vi,

23. "In this was manifested the love of God toward us, because that God sent His only begotten Son into the world, that we might live through Him."—1 Jno. iv, 9. "This life is *in His Son.*" Denying this would be denying "the record that God gave of His Son."—1 Jno. v, 10, 11. Hence He is called "our *life,*" and "the way, the truth, and the *life.*"—Col. iii, 4: Jno. xiv, 6. And that gift of eternal life is for none but a certain and specified class—"Thou hast given Him power over all flesh, that He should give eternal life to AS MANY AS THOU HAST GIVEN HIM."—Jno. xvii, 2. Hence He does not say that Adam transmitted to them eternal life, but "*I* give unto them eternal life, and they shall never perish."—Jno. x, 28. "God so loved the world that He gave His only begotten Son, that whosoever believeth in Him should not perish but have everlasting life."—Jno. iii, 16. The belief of this great truth enables us to properly and highly appreciate the great atonement and the precious blood poured out on the cross for us. It extols the sufferings and the divine love of our Saviour; and helps us to "give unto the Lord the glory due unto His name," as our Life-giver.—Psa. xcvi, 8. But it humbles the *carnal pride* of man by showing him that "we all do fade as a leaf" and that none of us are by nature immortal.

2. We have not yet obtained immortality, but it is a matter of promise, hope, and reward; and will

be given to none but those who properly "seek for" it. Proof: "This is the promise that He hath promised us even eternal life."—1 Jno. ii, 25. " In hope of eternal life . . . That being justified by His grace, we should be made heirs, according to the hope of eternal life."—Titus i, 2 ; iii, 7. " If thou wilt enter into life *keep* the commandments."—Mat. xix, 17. " They that have done *good* shall come forth unto the resurrection of life."—Jno. v, 29. "To them who by patient continuance in *well* doing SEEK FOR glory, honor and immortality," He will render eternal life.—Rom. ii, 7. " As righteousness tendeth to life, so he that pursueth evil pursueth it to his own death."—Prov. xi, 19: viii, 35, 36.

3. It is to be obtained in the resurrection, at the personal coming of Christ. Proof: "They that have done good shall come forth to the resurrection of life."—Jno. v, 29. Many that shall sleep in the dust of the earth shall awake to everlasting life.—Dan. xii, 2. When " the Lord himself shall descend from heaven " and the dead in Christ shall rise, "this mortal shall put on immortality."—1 Thess. iv, 16: 1 Cor. xv, 42, 54.

Remember the terms on which that everlasting life is to be obtained. You must believe in the Son of God. This means, as proved in the second discourse, a belief of the message, testimony or doctrine which He preached. It is a mistake to suppose that you truly believe in Him so long as you refuse to believe His word or doctrine. The vague notion that believing in the Son is something less than believing the Son, is a dangerous and delusive piece of sophistry. If any such quibble be raised about believing *in* the Son (ver. 16), John settles it in ver. 33 by showing the essentiality of believing the Son's *testimony;* and in v. 36 by saying, "He that believeth not the Son (no 'in' here) shall not see life; but the wrath of God abideth on him."—John iii, 33, 36. And so Paul, in a sublime sentence of three words, says, "I believe God," i. e. he believed what God had said.—Ac. xxvii, 25. Thus, too, "Abraham believed God," i. e. believed the promises which God had made to him.—Gal. iii, 6: Rom. iv, 21. And so in order to obtain eternal life *you* must be able to say, "I believe Jesus," i. e. believe the words that He preached—THE GOSPEL OF THE KINGDOM. And will you not commence *now* to seek for that immortality which the Redeemer died to purchase for you? If you had the wealth of Stewart, the power of the Czar of Russia, the strength of Samson, the wisdom of Solomon, and the long life of Methusaleh, but should come short of eternal life at last, your life would be a miserable failure, and you had better never have been born. But however humble your lot may now be, if you succeed in obtaining eternal life at the resurrection you will be unspeakably blest. You may regret having begun too late to seek for it, but surely you will never regret having begun too soon. Did you ever hear one on a death-bed regret having led a long and holy Christian life? O then, I beseech you, do not any longer " neglect so great salvation."

Look at three scenes in the sinner's career. 1. See him attentively and respectfully listening to the gospel of the kingdom, as its exceeding great and precious promises are explained concerning the coming of Christ, the establishing of that kingdom on earth, and the everlasting joys which the redeemed will then obtain therein. He listens to the invitations exhorting him to believe, be baptized, and lead a holy life, that he may be saved when that kingdom comes. Perhaps tears gather in his eyes as he listens, and he is *almost* persuaded to be a Christian; but, with a great struggle, he hardens his heart, resists the good influence, and, when the assembly is dissolved, he goes away sorrowful, because the love of sin has a deadly hold upon him.

2. Some time has passed; the scene is changed. Behold him prostrate on a bed of pain, groaning in the agonies of death; and oh! sad thought! he is dying *in his sins*. A young man, himself a sinner, having waited at the bedside of such a person, whose agony was too horrible to witness, declared to me at the breakfast table next morning, " I never want to see another sinner die." Yes, behold the sinner dying with *no* comfort in his

last hour, but only "a fearful looking for of the fiery indignation which shall devour the adversary."

3. See him in the resurrection, summoned from the grave and hurried before the great white throne of judgment. Pale and trembling, he stands to hear the awful sentence, and all in a moment his features appear to be pinched and shrunken, and I seem to hear some, standing by, say, "How soon is the fruitless tree withered away!" Then hear that haunting scream—his last, long, unearthly shriek of woe as he is cast headlong into the consuming billows of the "lake of fire."

But look at three scenes in the Christian's career. 1. Having confessed his belief of "the things concerning the kingdom of God and the name of Jesus Christ" (which things compose the gospel of the kingdom—Ac. viii, 12), and having been baptized for the remission of sins, he comes up out of the water enabled henceforth to rejoice in hope of the glory of God.

2. And when he comes to die, see the weeping friends around his bed; but on his own countenance is the mark of inward peace, for he knows that underneath are the everlasting arms, and he can say, "Though I walk through the valley of the shadow of death, I will fear no evil; for thou art with me, thy rod and thy staff they comfort

me."—Psa. xxiii. And so he passes quietly away like the summer wave upon the shore.

3. At last behold him in the resurrection morn; he stands among the shining ranks and sings the glad redemption song. He and all that host in bright array have come out of great tribulation, and have washed their robes and made them white in the blood of the Lamb. And so "they shall hunger no more, neither thirst any more; neither shall the sun light on them, nor any heat. For the Lamb who is in the midst of the throne shall feed them, and shall lead them unto living fountains of waters; and God shall wipe away all tears from their eyes."—Rev. vii, 14-17.

SEVENTH DISCOURSE.

THE SUBJECTS, NATURE, DESIGN, AND IMPORTANCE OF CHRISTIAN BAPTISM.

"He that believeth and is baptized, shall be saved."—
MARK xvi, 15, 16.

1. The subjects. From what the Bible says of households, an effort has been made to prove that infants are proper subjects of this ordinance. But of the three household baptisms brought forward to prove this we have evidence that two at least were *believing* households; for the jailor "re-

joiced, believing in God with *all* his house"; and the household of Stephanas "addicted themselves to the ministry of the saints."—Ac. xvi, 32, 34: 1 Cor. i, 16: xvi, 15. To prove that Lydia's household contained an infant we should have to take four things for granted which the Scripture is silent upon—that she was a married woman; that she had at least one child; that it was an infant; that it was with her at Philippi, and not at her home, which seems to have been in Thyatira, about 200 miles away. If an household may be spoken of as "believing," although containing an unbelieving infant, why may it not by the same license of speech be spoken of as "baptized," although containing an unbaptized infant? Many things can be said of a family or household to the exclusion of its infants; as, when we speak of "family prayer," no one imagines that the little infant in the cradle engages in it. "The man Elkanah and *all* his house" went to Shiloh to offer sacrifice, but the infant of the house was left at home with its mother.—1 Sam. i, 21, 22. "All the city was moved, saying, Who is this?" But although the city must have contained many households with infants, you would not suppose that every one of them stood up in its mother's lap and said, "Who is this?"—Mat. xxi, 10. "He that cometh to God must *believe*" (Heb. xi, 6), but infants cannot *come* to Him in that sense, being not yet capable of believing; and hence I think the Saviour used the word "come" in its ordinary or local sense of motion towards a person in whose presence you may be standing, when He said "Suffer the little children to come unto me." It is not said that He baptized them, but took them up and "blessed them."—Mark x, 16. It was towards the close of His ministry, and if He and John had for years been in the *habit* of baptizing infants, would not the disciples have rather encouraged than rebuked the parents for bringing their children? Certainly the officers of a modern infant-sprinkling church would feel it their duty to encourage them. If they had been brought for baptizing I think the Saviour would have said, "Carry them to my disciples," instead of "Suffer them to come unto *me*," for "Jesus himself baptized *not*." His disciples did *that*.—John iv, 2. So this incident serves rather to *refute* than prove infant baptism. All Christians are the children of Abraham (his multitudinous "seed"), but the new principle on which they are made his children, in the true and gospel sense, is faith followed by baptism; not mere natural birth, for "they which are of *faith*, the same are the children of Abraham. . . As many of you as have been *baptized* into Christ have put on Christ. . . and if ye be Christ's then are ye Abraham's seed, and heirs according to the promise."—Gal. iii, 7, 27, 29. A Gentile infant is therefore neither a child of Abraham by natural birth nor by the process of adoption just described. If deceased infants are to be saved when the Lord comes, and I truly hope they will; if it be His good pleasure, I say amen to it with all my heart. They will not be saved, however, by a present exercise of *faith*, for they are incapable of believing. If saved, then, I suppose it will be through the same abounding merits of the atonement, as the inanimate earth itself will be regenerated, and, as it were, resurrected into eternal glory and beauty. But the gospel and its ordinances are for those who have arrived at years of *accountability*, which means ability to give account; and unless all such persons believe and obey that gospel they will have to suffer the penalties. If baptism is for infants, why not the Lord's supper also? Was not that feast given for *all* the members of the Church when the Master said, " This do in remembrance of me. . . Drink *all* ye of it "? The " all " means all the members, not the wine; accordingly Mark says, " They *all* drank of it."—Mat. xxvi, 27: Mark xiv, 23: Lu. xxii, 19.

We have neither command nor example for infant sprinkling. Indeed the commission forbids it by requiring two kinds of teaching, one *before* and one *after* baptism, which would of course be impracticable in baptizing infants. Here is the language of the commission—" Go ye therefore and *teach* (*mathētueo*) all nations, baptizing them into (*eis*) the name of the Father, and of the Son, and of the Holy Spirit, *teaching* (*didasko*) them to observe all things whatsoever I have commanded you."—Matt. xxviii, 19, 20. * This commission is obeyed by none but those who give the two kinds of instruction—before baptism, the gospel of the kingdom; and after baptism "all things" that pertain to the duties of a Christian life. Matthew's record is confirmed in Mark's, "He that believeth and is baptized," not he that is first baptized and *afterwards* believeth, if he should live long enough.

And as the commands of Scripture are opposed to infant sprinkling, so are its examples. It tells us that "both *men* and *women*" were baptized, not men, women and *infants*.—Ac. viii, 12. They were capable of " confessing their sins," which infants are not.—Mat. iii, 12. They "gladly received the word" before baptism.—Acts ii, 41. "Many Corinthians hearing, believed, and were baptized."—Ac. xviii, 8. Here are the three steps exactly expressed "after the due order ": (1st) hearing; (2nd) belief; (3rd) baptism. And Paul afterwards charged the same church to keep the ordinances "*as*" he delivered them.—1 Cor. xi, 2.

---

* "Two words in this passage are translated teach and teaching, but are of different meaning. The former means the general instruction necessary to bring men to profess themselves disciples of Christ; the other relates to their subsequent instruction in all the various parts of Christianity." —Scott, the celebrated Episcopal Commentator.

Uzzah, no doubt, *meant* well, but his act was not "after the *due* order," and so he was not excused for ignorance or sincerity, but smitten dead; which things are "for *our* admonition."—1 Chron. xiii, 10; xv, 12–15; 1 Cor. x, 11. I hope I have now said enough on this branch of the subject to convince all with whom Holy Scripture has more weight than human tradition.

2. The nature of baptism. We prove baptism to be immersion by three lines of argument:—1st, The lexical definition of the Greek verb *baptizo;* 2nd, The symbols under which it is illustrated; 3d, The literal phrases used in describing the act. Greenfield's Lexicon says it means " to immerse, immerge, submurge;" Liddell and Scott's, " to dip under, to bathe." It is a significant fact that although it occurs about eighty times in the Greek New Testament the translators have not once dared to render it "sprinkle" or "pour." And in the Old Testament where the Greek version has *baptizo* the translators have "dipped"; "Then went he down and dipped (baptizo) himself seven times in Jordan."—2 Kin. v, 14. Though some talk as if pouring, dipping and sprinkling were the same in a ceremonial way, yet the Bible carefully discriminates between them thus, "The priest shall take some of the log of oil, and pour (cheo) it into the palm of his own left hand. And the priest shall dip (bapto) his right finger in the oil that is in his left hand, and shall sprinkle

(raino) of the oil with his finger seven times before the Lord."—Lev, xiv, 15, 16. Carson, renowned for his work on baptism, says, "Some have alleged that the termination *zo* makes *baptizo* a diminutive; but utterly without countenance from the practice of the language. Others have erred as far on the other side, and equally without authority make *baptizo* a frequentative."* But the symbols in which the act of baptism is pictured to us give it a fixedness of meaning by showing that it cannot mean less than *immersion*, nor more than *one* immersion.

Burial, resurrection, planting, and birth are four symbols which teach immersion so plainly as to render comment nearly superfluous. "We are *buried* with Him by baptism."—Rom. vi, 4.† On

---

* Oswald's Etym. Dict. shows that "*ize* or *ise* denotes *to make, to give;*" as, civil-*ize, to make* civil; character-*ize to give* a character; author-*ize, to give*, authority; apolog-*ize, to give* an apology; harmon-*ize, to give* harmony. Hence as bapt-*ism* means an immersion or dipping, bapt-*ize* would mean *to give* an immersion or dipping. "Frequentative and Intensive verbs," according to Kuhner's Greek Grammar, are such as end in *azo*, not *izo*.

† "Alluding to the *ancient* manner of baptizing by immersion."—Jno. Wesley. "This passage cannot be understood unless it be borne in mind that the primitive baptism was by immersion."—Conybeare & Howson. "This immersion being religiously observed by all Christians for *thirteen* centuries... it were to be wished that this custom might be again of general use."—Whitby. And yet all these writers practised sprinkling!

land we bury a body by putting it under the ground, at sea by putting it under the water; never by merely sprinkling a few particles of dust or water upon it. The burial of a person is an open attestation to friends and foes that such an one is dead to the life which was formerly led. So in the baptismal burial we throw a great mountain across the path we have come, leaving no way open for turning back or "looking back" for we are determined henceforth to "press *forward*." Thus we show to sinners whom we leave, and to Christians whom we join that we are "dead to sin" and should not and would not "live any longer therein." Sin itself is personified to Christians as an "old man" who has been "destroyed, that henceforth we should not serve sin" or be in bondage to him; for when a master is dead his servant no longer owes him any service. And this freedom is doubly secure for not only is the master dead to the servant, but the servant to the master, and "he (the servant) that died is freed from sin" or as Paul elsewhere says, "The world is crucified unto me, and I unto the world."—Rom. vi, 6, 7; Gal. vi, 14. Burial is a solemn thing; so also is baptism; but instead of the tears of sorrow at a grave we often see tears of joy at a baptism.

"Buried with Him in baptism, wherein also ye are *risen* with Him."—Col. ii, 12. Rising "out of the water" to walk in newness of life is a beautiful emblem of coming forth from the grave at the resurrection to walk in endless life and glory in the kingdom of God. As in baptism we "wash away" our sins and "put on Christ," so "in the the resurrection at the last day" we are freed from "this vile body" and are "clothed upon" with the shining and spotless robe of immortality. As one raised from the dead and exulting in all the holy joys of a blissful immortality will not desire to return to the former mortal fallible and suffering life, so neither should one raised from the baptismal grave desire to return to his former habits of worldliness and sin. By the baptismal act we show our faith in the death, burial and resurrection of Christ, and in His power to raise *us* from the dead, for He says, "Because I live ye shall live also." Will there be joy unspeakable as the glorified redeemed clasp hands in the resurrection? I have witnessed what seemed to me a foretaste of such joy when believers of the gospel of the kingdom have come up out of the baptismal wave. Often have I beheld, on such occasions, an overflowing joy that could find no expression but in tears. How impressive the solemn scene! Worldlings are encouraged to follow the holy example, and Christians reminded of the day of their own espousals when they went after the Saviour, as in the wilderness; and they are led to think of their own solemn engagements, and in what manner they have been fulfilled.

"*Planted* together in the likeness of His death."

—Rom. vi, 5. As a seed is covered up in the earth when planted in the ground, and afterwards springs forth to bloom and blossom into beauty, fragrance and fruitfulness, even so the believer is covered up in the baptismal wave, and emerges "a new creature," to "worship the Lord in the beauties of holiness," to shed forth the fragrance of Christian life, and, as a good tree, to become "filled with the fruits of righteousness which are by Jesus Christ, unto the glory and praise of God."

"*Born* of water."—Jno. iii, 5. As when born of the flesh we enter the world, so when believers of the gospel of the kingdom are born of water they enter the church "as newborn babes" who afterwards "grow in grace and in the knowledge of our Lord and Saviour Jesus Christ." This is not the only text in which natural birth is made a symbol of baptism, for the same is done in calling it "the washing of regeneration," i. e. of the "new birth," (as *paliggenesia* denotes); and in those texts which represent persons just baptized as "new creatures" or "newborn babes."—Titus iii, 5. In the phrases "born *of* the flesh" and born *of* water," the preposition is *ek*, which means "out of," and is so translated in Ac. viii, 39. How then can a man be born of water without first being *in* the water? This proves the necessity of immersion too plainly to need further comment.* It is not

---

* By the act of being *once* born an infant is ushered into a family relationship to *all* of its kindred. It is not born a

said "born of the Spirit and of water," but the water is put *first*. A believer is born of water at baptism, and afterwards born of the Spirit when by it "his mortal body" is quickened and brought forth ("born from the dead") at the resurrection. Col. i, 18; Rom: viii, 11. Such a body, though substantial, may be called "spirit" as to its nature, because it is no longer "a natural body" but "a spiritual body" physically "partaking of the *divine* nature,' and is fashioned like unto the glorious body of the risen Saviour who is called "a quickening *Spirit*" (1 Cor. xv, 45), although he had a substantial and tangible body in which could be felt the prints of the nails that pierced His hands on the cross. Thus the birth of water at baptism and the birth of the Spirit at the resurrection may be called the great law of naturalization necessary

separate time for each name in the family. And so in the one act of emerging from the water we are brought into a holy relationship to the *three* names Father, Son, and Spirit. Yes, in that *one* birth we even become related, in some degree to the whole family of redeemed, those who preceded and those who shall come after us. Hence it is plain that three dippings would do violence to this and each of the other symbols by which divine wisdom has pictured to us the grand old ordinance of "one baptism" (i. e. "one immersion."—A. B. U.) Eph. iv, 5. "The God of Abraham, and of Isaac, and of Jacob," does not means a separate God for each of those patriarchs; then why violate Scripture by saying that immersion into the name of the Father, and of the Son, and of the Holy Ghost, means a separate immersion for each of those holy names?

to take place on a man before he can obtain the immortal citizenship in the kingdom of God—a kingdom which flesh and blood cannot inherit.—1 Cor. xv, 50.

The literal terms used in describing the act of baptism also prove it to be immersion. How can " having our *bodies* washed with pure water" mean five drops of it sprinkled on the crown of the head?—Heb. x, 22. John baptized "*in the river*," and selected a particular place for it " because there was *much* water there."—Mat. iii, 6; Mar: 1, 5; John iii, 23. If John had offered his hearers their choice of three ways, occasionally (after the modern fashion) preaching a long tirade *against* immersion, think you that any of his hearers would have been immersed? Would they not *all* have chosen sprinkling or pouring as more convenient? And then we should never have read of their being "in the river." Such expressions as " went *down into* the water," and " came *up out of* the water," teach immersion too plainly to need comment.—Mar. i, 10; Acts viii, 38, 39. But some silly critic has said that "into the water" may mean only at or near by the water! How then about Noah's going " into the ark "; does this mean that he only got at or near by it, and saw it float off leaving himself and family to perish in the flood?—Gen. vii, 1. Daniel was cast " into the den of lions"; does that mean that he only went at or near by it, so as to get a safe view of them?—Daniel vi, 16-18.

Those who do His commandments will enter "into the city," would that critic dare to tell us that they will only get at or near by it, so as to just faintly hear the singing?—Rev. xxii, 14. Those not found written in the book of life will be "cast into the lake of fire," and does this mean only at or near by it, so as to merely be comfortably warm? It is the same preposition, *eis*, in the Greek of all these places. Has that preposition strength enough to take one into the consuming lake of fire but not enough to take him into the delightful waters of baptism? I hope I will be excused for answering that silly critic as I have done, for it seems to me that his extremely absurd criticism deserves only to be "fried in its own gravy," as the saying is. In a careless manner some say that a drop of water is as good as an ocean; but they would not say so if they wanted to quench a parching thirst. Hagar and her son wandered thirsty in the wilderness, and as she laid him down to die, and turned away and wept, the Lord showed her a whole well of water; one drop would not have saved those two lives. As in the Lord's supper, there must be enough bread and wine to constitute eating and drinking, so in baptism there must be at least enough water to constitute immersion. If immersion is right it ought not to be preached against, and if wrong it ought not to be practiced; but some preachers do *both*, for after a long sermon against it they have gone to the water and immersed people! There are two parties in the world: one claiming that either sprinkling, pouring, or immersion is right; the other that immersion only is right. Thus neither party disputes the correctness of immersion. In all candor then, does not common prudence commend immersion to you as the *safest* way?

3. The design of baptism. It is designed to change our state or relationship, conducting a believer "*into* the name," *eis* to onoma, of the Father, and of the Son, and of the Holy Spirit. Mat. xxviii, 19.* The common version has elsewhere rendered *eis*, "into," with reference to this ordinance, as "baptized into (*eis*) one body,"—1 Cor. xii, 13; "baptized into (*eis*) Christ,"—Gal. iii, 27; "baptized into (*eis*) His death,"—Rom. vi, 3. Bullion's Greek grammar says that *eis* is used to express motion from without to within; and that *en* is used with the idea of rest or being contained within. You were standing without, but walked *into* the house and were seated *in* the house. After Noah went "*into* (*eis*) the ark;" he was said to be "*in* (*en*) the ark" and all

---

* "*In* the name is a manifest mistranslation, the preposition in the original is not *en* but *eis, into* or *to*."—Archbishop Whately. "It should have been into (as in Gal. iii, 27). It imports an objective admission into the covenant of redemption—a putting on of Christ. Baptism is the contract of espousal (Ephes. v, 26) between Christ and His church."—Alford. "It should be 'into the name' as in 1 Cor. x, 2, and Gal. iii. 27."—*Commentary of Jamieson, Faussett & Brown.*

perished except those in the ark.—Gen. vii, 7, 23. After one believes the gospel of the kingdom and is "*baptized* into Christ" he is declared to be *in* "Christ;" and "if any man be in Christ he is a *new* creature." And as all in the ark were safe, so all in Christ are safe, provided they hold out faithful; for "there is therefore now no condemnation to them which are in Christ Jesus, who walk not after the flesh but after the Spirit."—Gal. iii, 27, 28; 2 Cor. v, 17; Rom. viii, 1. Suppose as Noah was entering the ark, some strong swimmer had said, "I'm just as good as some of that family; Noah is too exclusive and uncharitable in saying that nobody but he and those with him in the ark will be saved; I'll take my chances outside;" would such a course have saved that swimmer? No, nor will it save the modern scoffer who says he is as good as some in the church, refuses to be baptized into Christ, and trusts to his self-righteousness as the swimmer did to his own strength. I have spoken of a change of *state* or *relationship*. This is more than a mere change of the feelings. Let me illustrate this fact. Suppose two young ladies, on a very slight acquaintance with a young gentleman, have a strong aversion to him; but afterwards, on a better acquaintance, they both change their minds to such an extent as to cherish profound respect and affection for him; and shortly after, one of them, by the ceremony of marriage becomes his *wife*. They both changed their feelings, but only one changed her relationship to him. Two English gentlemen may be great enemies of this government and its principles; but afterwards change their minds, and become great lovers of it, insomuch that one of them, by submitting to the ceremony of naturalization, becomes an American citizen. Though both changed their feelings, only one changed his relationship towards this government, the other remained an alien still. So the sinner may change his feelings concerning religion, and may very much admire and love the Christian life, but still remains an alien until he submits to the ceremonial of being "baptized into Christ." In the act of baptism the believer passes from a state of condemnation to a state of pardon, which implies the remission of his sins that are past, and his becoming "a *new* creature." Hence baptism is expressly declared to be "for the REMISSION of sins;" and Paul was told to "be baptized and WASH AWAY his sins." ☞ If Paul, as the language implies, did not get rid of *his* past sins until baptism why think to get rid of yours *before* baptism? —Ac. ii, 38; xxii, 16. "For the remission of your sins" does not mean "because your sins are remitted," any more than a man would take medicine for a sickness because he was already well of it. When Naaman had the leprosy, a type of sin, did he baptize himself in Jordan for the cure of it because he was already cured, or did he get cured *in the act?* Certainly in the act of dipping.

'4. The importance of baptism. The fact that it is for the remission of sins proves it essential, for you must admit that we cannot be saved without that remission. The same phrase which denotes the object of baptism denotes the object for which the precious blood of Christ was shed— " for the remission of sins," *eis aphesin hamartiōn.* While this proves the importance of baptism, it does not show any conflict, but only a coöperation between the blood and the water in the means of salvation. It is the blood which gives *efficacy* to the water by divine appointment. " Baptism doth now save us *by* the resurrection of Jesus Christ," which includes the shedding of His BLOOD on the cross. 1 Pet. iii, 21. The breaking of a straw would have answered in the place of immersion if the *Lord* had so *appointed* it. Baptism, important as it is, will not save you without faith, repentance and holiness of life; nor would all these combined save you but for the atoning blood of Christ, for " without shedding of blood is no remission."— Heb. ix, 22. Thus every truth, every duty and every instrumentality has its proper place in the plan of redemption. It is no valid objection to say that what I have said about baptism makes the salvation of one person depend upon the willingness of another to baptize him, for if an instance could occur in which it would be *impossible* to get any one to baptize him, I am sure that a believer might baptize himself, as Naaman did. Besides, on the same principle, it might be objected that *faith* makes a man's salvation depend on some one else, for "faith cometh by hearing," and "how can they hear without a *preacher?*"—Rom. x, 14, 17; Heb. xi, 6. Refusing to be baptized is rejecting the counsel of God, like some wicked ones of old, and of course no one can be saved who rejects that counsel.—Lu. vii, 30; Prov. i, 24-33. Its being a divine *command* is enough to prove it essential. Cornelius, though "a devout man, and one that feared God with all his house, which gave much alms to the people, and prayed to God alway," was "*warned* from God" to send for Peter and hear words whereby he might "be *saved.*" And when Peter came he did not excuse that devout man from baptism; how then can you expect to be excused?—Ac. x and xi.* Since it was necessary for Cornelius and even for the pure and spotless Lamb of God to go down into the baptismal waters and come up, all dripping, from the waves, it would be utterly preposterous to say

---

* "Some in our day would have argued, 'These are baptized with the Holy Ghost, and therefore what need have they to be baptized with water? It is below them.' No; it is not below them while water baptism is an ordinance of Christ."—MATT. HENRY. "The baptism of the Spirit did not supercede the baptism by water; nor indeed can it."—ADAM CLARKE.

that it is not necessary for people in *these* days. The fate of many people was once decided by their dropping a letter in pronouncing a word. Let this warn us not to call baptism a small matter.— Judg. xii, 6. "Except a man be born of water and of the Spirit, he cannot enter the kingdom of God."—John iii, 5. Can we need a plainer or more solemn assurance of its importance? Why is the birth of Spirit essential to an entrance into the kingdom? Because God has ordained it so. And why is the birth of water also essential? For the same sovereign reason. "Even so, Father, for so it seemed good in thy sight."

The mere possibility that the ceremony which you do not remember, and which was performed on you in infancy, was *no* baptism, ought to alarm you. It is said, I know not how truly, that on that fearful night in Egypt when the first-born was slain in every house which had no blood on the doorpost, a little girl, the first-born of the family, was sick; and in her fever she thought that perhaps the blood was not on the doorpost. So she asked her father if he was *sure* it was there; and her father said "Yes, he was sure, for he had ordered it to be done." But as it wore on towards the solemn hour of midnight, and her fever grew no better but rather worse, she said, "Father, take me up in your arms and carry me to the door, and let me *see* the blood." And so the father took her up and carried her to the door;

and lo and behold! the blood was *not there;* the man to whom he had given instructions had forgotten to do it! And then the father, in the sight of his daughter, had the blood put upon the doorpost; and she laid down quiet and contented. Can you be satisfied until you have SEEN your baptism? Those who think their having been sprinkled in infancy is enough ought to remember that under the Mosaic law grown persons who had been both circumcised and sprinkled were required to "*bathe in water,*" and for neglecting it a man had to "bear his iniquity."—Lev. xvii, 15, 16; Num. xix, 7, 8, 19. Of how much sorer punishment shall he be thought worthy who neglects the bathing which Christ has commanded? Why take it for granted that the penitent thief had never been baptized? Perhaps he was one of the vast multitude baptized by John, and "willing for a *season* to rejoice in his light."—John v, 35. That he was no ordinary thief is shown by his wonderful intelligence in acknowledging the Messiah, whom so many others had deserted. James indicates that such a thing as the restoration of a penitent brother is not impossible, by saying, "Brethren, if any of *you* do err," &c.—Jas. v, 19, 20. Besides, it seems that the gospel ordinances were not fully established in place of the Mosaic before the death and resurrection of Christ. "He taketh away the first that He may establish the second."—Heb. x, 9. Beware of undervaluing bodily acts. Was it not a bodily act when Eve reached forth her hand and plucked and ate of the forbidden fruit, and so brought death into the world, and all our woe? Was it not a bodily act when Christ, the spotless Lamb of God, was nailed to the cross and His body pierced for our sins? Was it not a bodily act when He arose from the dead, without which our faith would be vain?— 1 Cor. xv, 17. And will not our final redemption be a bodily act; "waiting for the adoption, to-wit: the redemption of our body"?—Romans viii, 23: Phil. iii, 21. How infinitely more delightful to go down into the baptismal waters and come out again, than to be cast into the lake of fire and be consumed into *ashes*!—Mal. iv, 3; Rev. xx, 15. Oh, *can* you hesitate which to choose?

[From "Songs of Zion." By WILEY JONES.]

Saviour thy law we love,
  Thy pure example plead;
And faith sincere, by works we prove
  When in thy steps we tread.

Beneath the sacred wave
  The Lord of life was laid;
And He who came to bless and save,
  Did not this path evade.

He taught the solemn way;
  He fixed the holy rite.
He bade us that command obey,
  And keep the path of light.

May ev'ry action show
  Our rev'rence for thy word;
And thus the world around shall know
  We love and serve the Lord.

EIGHTH DISCOURSE.

CHRISTIAN DUTIES AND GRACES TO BE OBSERVED AND CULTIVATED AFTER BAPTISM.

"Giving all diligence, *add* to your faith virtue; and to virtue knowledge; and to knowledge temperance; and to temperance patience; and to patience godliness; and to godliness brotherly kindness; and to brotherly kindness charity."—2 PETER i. 5-7.

To suppose that any man can be saved for general correctness of moral character without any reference to his faith would be a dreadful mistake. The words "*add* to your faith" prove that the faith must *first* be had as an essential foundation or starting point; and that all the shining list of Christian virtues are things to be *added* to it. Correct faith is as needful as correct conduct. (Remember what an excellent man was Cornelius; and yet he had to hear words of doctrine and be baptized, in order to place himself in a *salvable* state.—Acts x, 2; xi, 14.) The exhortation is addressed to those who have obtained like precious faith with the apostles; verse 1. Having believed the gospel of the kingdom, as preached by the apostles, and having been baptized, they are now, as the commission requires, exhorted to the duties which follow baptism.—Mat. xxviii, 19. These two features of the commission—giving the one kind of instruction before and the other after baptism—the apostles constantly observed. Thus Peter begins and ends this list of virtues by urging them upon those who had been baptized. And Paul desired Titus to " affirm *constantly* that they which have believed in God might be careful to maintain *good* works."—Titus iii, 8. James too has warned his brethren that " faith without *works* is dead."—Jas ii, 20. And thus the beloved disciple, after assisting in planting many churches, when he found himself too old to travel and visit them any longer, wrote to them as to his own dear children, saying, " I have no greater *joy* than to hear that my children walk in truth."—3 Jno. 4. No wonder it gave John so much joy to hear this, for our labor in preaching the gospel is, to a great extent, lost unless the converts, after baptism, continue to " walk in the truth." We naturally feel an interest in the success and prosperity of any undertaking on which we have spent much labor and care. Congregations which have displayed great and worthy zeal to have the gospel of the kingdom preached, and sinners converted, should show a similar zeal to build up and keep those converts in their most holy faith, continually exhorting them unto love and to good works; the older brethren and sisters especially taking care to live so as to set holy examples to the flock.—1 Pet. v, 3; Titus ii, 7. The Master's words, " What do ye more than others?" indicate that He requires Christians to be " a *peculiar* people *zealous* of good works." They are the conserving and illuminating element of society—the *salt* of the earth and the *light* of the world.—Mat. v, 13, 14, 47. "If ye *continue* in my word, then are ye my disciples indeed."—Jno. viii, 31. He that heareth and *doeth* is likened unto a wise man that built his house on a rock; unto good ground that bringeth forth an hundred fold; unto a fruitful branch of a goodly vine.—Mat. vii, 24; Lu. viii, 35; John xiv, 2, 6. But he that doeth not is like a foolish man that built his house on the sand; like thorny ground that chokes the seed; like a withered branch that is gathered and burned. Therefore "be ye *doers* of the word, and not hearers only."—Jas. i, 22. When the seven graces here enjoined, and all their kindred virtues are possessed in due proportion they give to the Christian a beautiful and symmetrical character.

1. Virtue. The gospel found the Gentiles fearfully sunk in vice, as the first chapter of Romans proves. Nor were the Jews, under Pharisaic teaching, free from rebuke in this respect. But Christians, to whom Peter was writing, had been " called to glory and virtue," and had "purified their souls in obeying the truth."—2 Pet. i, 3; 1 Pet. i, 22. They were tenderly exhorted, " Having therefore these promises, dearly beloved, let us cleanse ourselves from all filthiness of the flesh and spirit, perfecting holiness in the fear of God."—2 Cor. vii, 1. If this word, *aretē*, be translated " fortitude," as some

say, it then means that we must not only believe the gospel of the kingdom, but have the courage to confess it before men; for if ashamed of the Saviour's words (among which were "the glad tidings of the kingdom," Lu. viii, 1), He will be ashamed of us when He comes in glory.—Lu. ix, 26. We should be "valiant for the truth" (Jer. ix, 3), for "the fearful" are classed among the unbelieving and abominable who shall be cast into the lake of fire.—Rev. xxi, 8. This condemned fear is the fear of *man*, which "bringeth a snare;" not the fear of the Lord, for *that* " is the beginning of wisdom."—Prov. xxix, 25; Psa. cxi, 10. Who would not rather burn at the stake for righteousness than in the lake of fire for sin? The fear of man causes persons to not only neglect religious duties, through dread of hurting their fortunes or of making enemies, but even to abandon the faith. Too fond of popularity or too timid, they always drift with the current; reminding one of the saying that *dead* fish float down the stream. In Turkey they would perhaps be Mohammedans. They cannot "dare to be a Daniel, dare to stand alone, dare to have a purpose firm and dare to make it known." *He* would not be restrained from worshipping the true God by the dread of the lion's den; nor would His three companions be constrained to idolatry by the terrors of a fiery furnace. Of holy fortitude, duly combined with and tempered by all the other graces, the blessed

Saviour's life on earth is a perfect illustration.— 1 Pet. ii, 21.

2. Knowledge. Some "being alienated from the life of God through the ignorance that is in them," will be "destroyed for lack of knowledge." Ephes. iv, 18; Hos. iv, 6. This does not mean worldly "science," but a knowledge of the Scriptures, enabling us to understand for ourselves and to teach others "what the will of the Lord is."— Ephes. v, 17. Such knowledge enables its possessor to give a right direction to his fortitude— when he strives, it is "to enter in at the straight gate;" when he contends, it is "for the faith once delivered to the saints;" when he provokes, it is "unto love and to good works." He learns to rightly divide the word of truth, comparing Scripture with Scripture. He avoids "foolish and unlearned questions, and strivings about words to no profit but to the subverting of the hearers." He is not carried about by every wind of doctrine, nor persuaded into the belief of error by the smooth words and fair speeches, nor the high-sounding titles and arrogant pretensions of men. And with all this he is not haughty nor puffed up against those brethren who have not made the same attainments as himself, because any such disposition is restrained by his brotherly kindness, which he is also careful to cultivate.

3. Temperance. The Greek word implies moderation, continence, self-control. There are

many kinds of intemperance. *Ne quid nimis*, not anything too far, is with remembering. "Every man that striveth for the mastery is temperate in *all* things."—1 Cor. ix, 25. Now if the self-denial, abstemiousness, and severe exercises of the ancient contestants in public games were cheerfully endured in order to obtain a corruptible crown, the failure to obtain which would only be a temporary disgrace, how much more cheerfully ought we to endure all things in order to obtain an incorruptible crown, the failure to obtain which will bring "shame and everlasting contempt."—Dan. xii, 2. Paul's contest was not a beating of air, for in himself he found a more substantial antagonist—"I keep *my* body under, and bring *it* in subjection." We must "mortify," that is, put to death evil propensities, or they will be likely to put us to death. Many, to all their faith, fortitude, and knowledge have neglected to add temperance; and so at last have sunk to a drunkard's grave. O! the *inexpressible* wretchedness produced by that one vice! The heart-rending scenes and blighted home circles which the demon of drunkenness, has caused are enough to make it universally hated as a foe to the human race. It is well-known that it blunts the moral sensibilities, dulls the intellect, empties the purse, ruins the health, and at last excludes its victim from the joys of a blissful eternity; for no drunkard "shall inherit the kingdom of God." 1 Cor. vi, 10. The fact that the doses of alcoholic drinks require in so many cases to be continually increased in quantity appears to me an indication that as common beverages they must be unwholesome; for water, milk, and even tea or coffee do not require to be increased in that unnatural way. Fishes are not drowned in water, nor troubles in strong drink, for "at the last it biteth like a serpent, and stingeth like an adder."—Prov. xxiii, 29, 30, 32. But the Church is the only "Temperance society" needed by a Christian. If the influences of religion do not restrain one from insobriety, I see not how any outside organization can.

4. Patience. "In your patience possess ye your souls."—Lu. xxi, 19. "Ye have need of patience, that, after ye have done the will of God, ye might receive the promise. For yet a little while, and He that shall come will come."—Heb. x, 36, 37. "Let patience have her perfect work." Jas. i, 4. "Fret not thyself in *any* wise to do evil."—Psa. xxxvii, 8. "The ornament of a *meek and quiet* spirit is, in the sight of God, of great price."—1 Pet. iii, 4. "Ye have heard of the patience of Job."—Jas. v, 11. It ought to be a sufficient encouragement to know that the Lord has said, "I will never leave thee nor forsake thee."—Heb. xiii, 5.

In trials and troubles 'tis heaven's design
Our dross to consume, our gold to refine.

5. Godliness. This grace throws a sacred lustre over the entire conduct, and "is profitable unto all things, having promise of the life that now is, and of that which is to come."—1 Tim. iv, 8. Piety and devotion are some of its meanings. It leads us to take delight in frequent prayer. The wording of the Lord's prayer indicates that it is to be used, not yearly, monthly, or weekly, but daily—"Give us *this day* our daily bread." When the Saviour said that men "ought always to pray and not to faint," He gave two illustrations, one teaching *perseverance* and the other *humility* in prayer.—Lu. xviii, 1-14. We should not be content with mere prayerful thoughts at irregular times, but should observe both the spirit and *posture* of prayer, by at least once every day kneeling and offering up, through Christ, our thanks and supplications to our Heavenly Father. That kneeling is the most usual posture is evident from the fact that Paul uses the expression, " I bow my knees," as but another way of saying, " I pray."—Ephes. iii, 14. Thus Peter, Paul, Daniel, Solomon, and even the adorable Redeemer himself used to pray.—Ac. ix, 40; xxi, 5; Dan. vi, 10; 2 Chron. vi, 13; Lu. xxii, 41. David and Daniel prayed "three times a day."—Dan. vi, 10; Psa. lv, 17. Godliness prompts us to a regular attendance at the Lord's supper, to commemorate with ever-grateful hearts the sufferings which He endured for our sakes. This virtue

kindles in us a fervent zeal for the advancement of religion and the prosperity of the cause of Christ; weaning us from worldliness and placing our affections on holy things; leading us to "abhor that which is evil and cleave unto that which is good." It implies also a performance of the duties we owe to our fellow creatures.

6. Brotherly kindness (Greek, *philadelphia*). In other passages this word is translated "brotherly love," or "love of the brethren." Love of kind is common to men and brutes. Even "birds of a feather flock together." Both in sound and sense we can trace a relationship between kin, kind, kindness. It is human to be humane. Love to the brethren is an evidence of our discipleship. "By this shall all men know that ye are my disciples, if ye have love one to another."— John xiii, 34, 35. It is an evidence that we have entered the Christian life. "We know that we have passed from death unto life, because we love the brethren. He that loveth not his brother abideth in death." It is an evidence that we love God. "Whoso hath this world's good, and seeth his brother have need, and shutteth up his bowels of compassion from him, how dwelleth the love of God in him?"—1 John iii, 14, 17. "He that loveth not his brother whom he hath seen, how can he love God whom he hath not seen?"—1 John iv, 20. It is the Saviour's new commandment—" A new commandment I give unto you,

that ye love one another."—John xiii, 34. It prompts us to "bear one another's burdens and so fulfill the law of Christ."—Gal. vi, 2. No need of "benevolent societies" for the members of a congregation where brotherly love abounds. They need not go to those worldly institutions as though the Church of Christ were not sufficient for the temporal as well as the eternal needs of man. Loving brethren will speak often one to another, and will not be likely to forsake the assembling of themselves together.—Mal. iii, 16. "Behold how good and how pleasant it is for brethren to dwell together in unity!" "Let brotherly love continue."—Psa. cxxxiii, 1; Heb. x, 25; xiii, 1.

7. Charity, or rather "*love*," as the A. B. U. renders it. Thus Peter exhorts us to love not our brethren *only*, but, as Paul expresses it, to "increase and abound in love one toward another, and toward *all* men."—Mat. v, 46; 1 Thes. iii, 12. This is not the mere giving of alms, for a person may give all his goods to feed the poor, and "*have not* charity" or love; in which case his almsgiving "profiteth nothing." Nor is it a blindness to the errors and false doctrines of others for charity or love "rejoiceth not in *iniquity*, but rejoiceth in the *truth*."—1 Cor. xiii, 3, 6. The two duties—charity and earnestly contending for the faith—would not be enjoined upon us if they were incompatible and contrary to one another. None have been more perfect examples of *true*

charity than Christ and His apostles, and yet they died contending against errors of doctrine and practice. Thousands of the early Christians were slain for their unflinching advocacy of the true faith, but if they had worn the modern garb of a false "charity," might they not have compromised with their opponents, and thus lived as completely at peace with them as the greatest moral coward or popularity seeker of the nineteenth century? All classes of errorists might be fellowshipped by sacrificing the truths and duties which the Bible teaches; but this, instead of resembling Christ and His apostles, would resemble Pilate and Herod, who made friends with one another in condemning Christ. As long as the word of God is held in proper value and esteem, there *must be* disputes and divisions among men.—Mat. x, 34. What remedy is there for it in the present condition of the world, which is not infinitely worse than the disease? A total *indifference* about all the teachings of the Bible would indeed end all disputes about it; but that indifference would be punished by the consuming wrath of God, in the day of judgment. It is a loving action to warn one who is in danger, even if you get no thanks for it. The Psalmist calls the reproof of the righteous a *kindness* and an *excellent oil*, and Solomon says, "As an earring of gold, and an ornament of fine gold, so is a wise reprover upon an obedient ear."—Psa. cxli, 5; Prov. xxv, 12. We must avoid casting pearls before swine, however.—Mat. vii, 6. After the Jews in a certain place had heard and *rejected* the word, Paul said, "It was necessary that the word of God should first have been spoken to you; but seeing ye put it from you, and judge yourselves unworthy of eternal life, lo, we turn to the Gentiles."—Ac. xiii, 45, 46. And so after one has manifested hatred and contempt for "the word of the kingdom," let us turn to others, in hopes of finding better and more hospitable soil for that precious word.—Mat. xiii, 19.

"Love worketh no ill to his neighbor."—Rom. xiii, 10. Hence the Christian refuses to arm himself with carnal weapons and slay his fellow man upon the battle-field. The disciples were reproved for quoting an instance under a *former* dispensation to justify *them* in slaying their enemies. Every Christian should be imbued with the same disposition as his Master who did "not come to destroy men's lives but to save them"—"let this mind be in you which was also in Christ Jesus."—Lu. ix, 56; Phil. ii, 5; 1 Jno. ii, 6; 2 Tim. ii, 24. "Render unto Caesar the things which are Caesar's," refers to *taxes*.—Mat. xxii, 21. The money bore the image of Caesar and was to be rendered to him; but the Christian bears the image of God, has been "*bought* with a price," and his body belongs to God by an infinitely better right than the money to Caesar; hence he is to glorify God in his *body*, and to render his body, blood, and life to God alone.—1 Cor. vi, 19, 20; Rom. xii, 1. Love is beautifully analyzed by Paul in 1 Cor. xiii. It is the crowning of Christian virtues, and is the only acceptable principle of obedience, whether under the law or the gospel. "Thou shalt love the Lord thy God with all thy heart, and with all thy soul, and with all thy mind. This is the *first* and *great* commandment. And the second is like unto it, Thou shalt love thy neighbor as thyself. On these two commandments hang all the law and the prophets."—Mat. xxii, 37, 40.

I have scarcely given more than a few seed-thoughts on the duties and graces of the Christian life. If we believe and advocate the gospel, and illustrate it in our lives, we will fully accomplish our mission,* for others beholding our good

---

* Each dispensation, systematically, has had its *beginning* and *foundation* laid in miracles; the Patriarchal in the miracles of creation and of Eden; the Mosaic in the miracles of the Exode and the conquest of Canaan; and the present dispensation in the miracles of Christ and His apostles. Prophets and apostles wrought miracles to confirm their words as a part of the volume of revelation; but when the Bible became a *completed* book, to which we dare not add (Rev. xxii, 18), miracles were discontinued, as the scaffolding used in constructing a building is taken down when the building is finished. Hence in *this* part of the gospel dispensation men are not to claim apostolic powers. The prediction in Mark xvi, 17, 18 was *fulfilled* in the *apostolic* age and ministry. Mark who wrote A.D. 65, towards the close of that ministry, actually records its fulfillment in v. 20—"the Lord working with them and confirming the word with THE SIGNS, *toon semeioon*, following."

works will glorify our Heavenly Father (Mat. v, 16), we will put to silence the ignorance of foolish men (1 Pet. ii, 15), and finally obtain an abundant entrance into the everlasting kingdom of our Lord and Saviour Jesus Christ." O glorious destiny! O blissful fruition of all our hopes and labors! Therefore, brethren and sisters, "keep yourselves in the love of God, looking for the mercy of our Lord Jesus Christ unto eternal life;" yea, "be ye steadfast, unmovable, always abounding in the work of the Lord, forasmuch as ye know that your labor is not in vain in the Lord." Jude 21; 1 Cor. xv, 58.

And sinner, why do you linger in a land of dragons? I beseech you to escape for your life to the gate of safety that kindly stands ajar for thee. In the book of life there is yet room for your name, and the door of mercy is not yet closed. O let me urge you to enter that door and have your name enrolled in that book ere it be too late. I've heard that on one occasion a speaker was dwelling on the danger of being shut out from salvation, and illustrating it by the closing of the ark; and as he described the great doors moving on their hinges, about to be closed, a lady in the audience intensely thinking of the scene cried out in anguish, Oh! *do* not close the door until *my husband gets in!* And is there not some one here to-day who is safe in the Ark but has a dear friend or relative still standing without and liable to be swept away by the coming waves of God's wrath? Ask them to begin *to-day* to seek the kingdom of God. I'll excuse you if you get up and go across the house to ask them. Let the mother speak to the daughter at her side, the father to his son, the wife to her husband; for the Lord will have a whole family to be saved—" come thou and *all thy house* into the ark." Soon the door will no longer stand open, the church will be caught away to meet the Lord, as the ark was borne away on the waters. No more invitations then, no more sermons, no more loving friends pleading with you to be saved, and to behold the Lamb of God. All this will be passed, the hour of judgment will have come and sinners of all classes great and small, high and low, will run terror stricken to rocks and mountains crying out " Fall on us and hide us from the face of Him that sitteth on the throne and from the *wrath* of the Lamb, for the *great* day of His *wrath* is come and *who* shall be able to stand."

A blooming young lady of Norfolk was walking the street as bright, healthy and cheerful as anybody in this house apparently, but was suddenly taken down sick and though surrounded by wealth and loving attentions of a multitude of friends, and ministered to by some of the best medical talent in the city she lingered but a few days, and then in spite of all that wealth and love and skill could do she *died*, and her death seemed to cast a gloom over nearly half the city. And I was told that she was engaged to be married and was literally shrouded in her bridal robes! Thus her wedding ceremony was a funeral sermon, her wedding dress a shroud, and her bridal chamber the grave! O sad, sad fate! Will you not let this warn you of the uncertainty of life? In the same city I knew a man who was making money rapidly and investing it in real estate, and though but middle aged he was taken down with some sudden disease and died in about twenty-four hours, and worse than all, died in his sins, for he was a notoriously wicked man.

I could relate many more such circumstances that have come within my own personal knowledge, but I forbear. Are not these enough to warn you of the uncertainty of life? O come to Jesus; come to-day. To the youthful, God says, "Remember *now* thy Creator in the days of thy youth;" to the aged, "Why stand ye here idle *all* the day?" See! the sun in the west; your white locks are blooming for the grave! O will you not go *now*, at the *eleventh* hour, and work in the vineyard? Better go late as this than not go at all.

Think not that you are naturally immortal, and that if you persist in sin you can outlive your future punishment, serve out your term, and finally enter the joys of the redeemed. Flatter not yourself with such vain hopes; for that which is immortal cannot die, " but the *soul* that sinneth it *shall* die"; hence the soul of the sinner is not immortal.—Eze. xviii, 4, 20. There will never be another moment of joy for those who die in their sins. Therefore, "*make haste* and *delay not* to keep the *commandments* of the Lord."—Psa. cxix, 60. He commands you to *believe the gospel of the kingdom,* and then "*be baptized and wash away your sins.*"—Mar. i, 14, 15; Ac. xxii, 16. Surely " His commandments are not grievous," but His yoke is easy and His burden light.—1 John v, 3.

[From "Songs of Zion."]

Behold an open door!
  It stands ajar for thee!
For thee, poor sinner, to secure
  Bless'd immortality.

The Saviour calls from sin,
  And bids you enter there;
'Tis life, and light, and joy within,
  And bliss beyond compare.

When closed by His command,
  Your tears may stain the sill,
But yet that door will ever stand
  Fast barr'd against you still.

'Tis mercy's only gate
  That leads to life and home;
Then hasten, ere it be too late,
  And flee from " wrath to come."

NINTH DISCOURSE.

THE KINGDOM AS DISTINGUISHED FROM THE CHURCH. A FEW PROMINENT SIGNS THAT THE KINGDOM IS NEAR.

"Thy Kingdom *come*. Thy will be done in *earth* as it is in *heaven*."—MATT. vi, 10.

In previous discourses I have shown that the kingdom of which the gospel speaks will *hereafter* be established on earth. But many hold the notion that the church itself is the kingdom. And this although they are expressed by two words which differ as much in Greek as in English. Church is *ekklesia*, kingdom is *basileia*. Ekklesia occurs about one hundred and fifteen times in the New Testament but is never translated *kingdom*. Basileia occurs about one hundred and sixty times but is never translated *church*. If they were the same ought they not, like other synonyms, to interchange and make sense? But see how strange and unscriptural it would sound to substitute *church* for kingdom in the following sentences. A *kingdom* that shall consume all these *kingdoms*.—Dan. ii, 44. The saints shall take the *kingdom* and possess the *kingdom*; (the saints themselves are the church; will the *church* take the *church?*). Dan. vii, 18. The time came that the saints possessed the *kingdom*.—Dan. vii, 22. "Inherit the *kingdom* prepared for you."—Mat. xxv, 34. "There shall be weeping and gnashing of teeth when ye shall see Abraham, and Isaac, and Jacob, and all the prophets in the *kingdom* of God, and you yourselves thrust out."—Lu. xiii, 28. "Sit down with Abraham, and Isaac, and Jacob in the *kingdom*."—Mat. viii, 8. "Who shall judge the quick and the dead at His appearing and His *kingdom*."—2 Tim. iv, 1. "Thy *kingdom* come." (Could the church pray for *itself* to come?) Mat. vi, 10. But among those who suppose the kingdom to be already in the world there is a wide difference of opinion as to the time when it was set up, some say on the first Pentecost after the Saviour ascended, others a great while before that. The latter class base their opinions, it seems, on a misunderstanding of such expressions as the following, used before Pentecost: "The kingdom of God is preached and every man presseth into it"—Lu. xvi, 16; "Ye shut up the kingdom of heaven against men; for ye neither go in yourselves, neither suffer ye them that are entering to go in" Mat. xxiii, 13; "The kingdom of God is come upon you"—Lu. xi, 20. A. Campbell, of Bethany, Va., taught that the kingdom was not set up until the day of Pentecost. I will therefore let him answer the preceding objections. He says, "Because Christ was promised and prefigured in the patriarchal and Jewish ages, the Paidobaptists will have the kingdom of heaven on earth since the days of

Abel; and because the glad tidings of the reign and kingdom of heaven and the principles of the new and heavenly order of society were promulged by John, the Baptists will have John the Baptist in the kingdom of heaven, and the very person who set it up. . . The *principles* of any reign or revelation are always promulgated, debated and canvassed before a new order of things is set up. . . In society, as in nature, we have first the blade, next the stem, and then the ripe corn in the ear. We call it wheat, or we call it corn, when we have only the *promise* in the blade. By such a figure of speech the kingdom of God was spoken of, while as yet only its *principles* were promulging. Jesus often unfolded its character and design in various similitudes, and every one who received these *principles* were said to 'press into the kingdom' or to have ' the kingdom within them ;' and wherever these principles were promulged 'the kingdom of heaven' was said to have 'come nigh' to that people, or to 'have overtaken them ;' and those who opposed these principles and interposed their authority to prevent others from receiving them, were said to ' shut the kingdom of heaven against men ;' and thus all those Scriptures must of necessity be understood from the contexts in which they stand. . . In *anticipation*, they who believed the gospel of the kingdom received the kingdom of God, just as in anticipation He said, 'I have finished the work which thou gavest me to do,' before He began to suffer; and as He said, 'This cup is the new testament in my blood, shed for the remission of the sins of many,' before it was shed... Those who received these principles by *anticipation* were said to enter the kingdom."—"Christian System," 1839, pp. 171–174. But that writer did not carry this principle of interpretation to its proper length, for the *same* kind of expressions used *after* Pentecost, such as "hath translated us unto the kingdom," or "your companion in the kingdom" must be understood in the *same* way, that is, as said by a figure of speech called prolepsis or *anticipation*; for I shall presently bring an overwhelming array of expressions which prove the actual setting up of the kingdom and the actual entrance therein to be *future*.

For convenience let us collect these testimonies into, 1st, those which prove that the kingdom was not set up *before* Pentecost; and 2d, those which prove it was not set up *at* Pentecost, and will not be set up before the second coming of the Lord Jesus.

I. Testimonies which prove that the kingdom was not set up *before* Pentecost. (1), John the Baptist said, "The kingdom of heaven is at hand," or "the reign of heaven *approaches*."—Campbell's edition, 1832, Mat. iii, 2. At hand does not mean "has come," but refers to *future* things, as "The end of all things is at hand," which, being said 1,800 years ago, proves that the expression can have a very wide scope.—1 Pet, iv, 7. See also Deut. xxxii, 35. Thus towards the close of this dispensation, on the very verge of the second advent, the kingdom is spoken of not as having come long before, but as being " still *at hand*— " When ye see these things come to pass, know ye that the kingdom of God is *nigh at hand.*"—Lu. xxi, 31. That cry, "the kingdom of God is at hand," extends over the whole present dispensation until it is fulfilled in the actual coming of the kingdom. The Saviour and His apostles likewise declared the kingdom to be *at hand.*—Mat. iv, 17; x, 7; Mark i, 15. What Matthew calls " the kingdom of heaven," the other evangelists, in reciting the same parables and incidents, call " the kingdom of God." (2). "He that is least in the kingdom of God is greater than John."—Lu. vii, 28. Hence John was not in the kingdom, though certainly " in the church," as was Moses in former times.— Ac. vii, 38. This proves that one can be in the church without being in the kingdom. If the church were the kingdom, you would have to believe that the *least* in the church was greater than John, of whom the Saviour said there was not a greater prophet " among those that are born of women." After sprinkling a few drops of water on the face of an infant, the Episcopal service says, "This child is now regenerate and grafted into the body of Christ's church." But can you suppose the Saviour to mean that the least and worst little infant sprinkled in this way is greater than John? I dare not so torture His words, but understand Him to say that the least immortal and glorified saint in the kingdom will be greater than John then was, in his mortal state; and at once the beauty and fitness of His words are seen. And those Jews who were too carnal and groveling in their ideas of that kingdom which the Messiah was foretelling, were, by this declaration of His, made to receive a more exalted conception of the nature and glory of it. "Is greater than John" means "shall be greater." It is the prospective present, as "They *are* equal to the angels," i. e. they *shall be* equal to them after the future resurrection.—Lu. xx, 36. (3). "Except your righteousness shall exceed the righteousness of the Scribes and Pharisees, ye shall in no case enter into the kingdom."—Mat. v, 1, 20. This was said to those who had become His disciples, and it proves that neither had *they* yet entered the kingdom. (4). "Seek ye the kingdom of God."—Lu. xii, 22, 31, 32. This too was said to the disciples—the "little flock"—but why tell them to seek it if they had already found it and were in it? (5). Pray ye "Thy kingdom come."—Mat. vi, 10. But why pray for it to come, if it had already come? Tertullian, who wrote near the end of the second century, shows that this prayer was used by Christians in his time, and that he did not regard the kingdom as having already come; for he says, in commenting on this petition, "Our wish is that our *reign* be hastened, not our servitude protracted. Even if it had not been prescribed in the prayer that we should ask for the *advent of the kingdom*, we should, unbidden, have sent forth that cry, hastening toward the realization of our hope."—On Prayer, ch. v. (6). Joseph was already "a disciple of Jesus," and yet he was "*waiting for* the kingdom."—John xix, 38; Lu. xxiii, 51—A. B. U. The participle is in the present tense, prosdechomenos, "waiting"; and in Titus ii, 13, is translated "looking for." It would be quibbling to say that he was still waiting for it because he was an *unworthy* church member; for this is at once refuted by the strong certificate of Scripture that he was "a *good* and *just* man."—Lu. xxiii, 50. Can you suppose that the kingdom was in the hearts of the wicked Pharisees but not in the heart of Joseph! If the kingdom only means grace ruling in the heart, that kingdom must have been on earth ever since Abel; for I do not see how any man from his time until now could be righteous unless grace ruled in his heart. Instead of "the kingdom of God is *within you*," the margin reads "the kingdom of God is *among* you."—Lu. xvii, 21. The word *basileia*, rendered "kingdom," also means "royal dignity" (see Greenfield's Lexicon), and this royal dignity is embodied in Christ, "in whom dwelleth all the fullness of the Godhead bodily," and in whom all the promises concerning that kingdom are, yea and amen. This metonymy of speech had been used in Dan. vii, 17, 23, in which a king is put for a kingdom; the fourth one of the "four kings" in ver. 17 is called "the fourth *kingdom*" in ver. 23. Thus the meaning would be, "The *King* is among you." By a similar metonymy He said, "I am the *resurrection*." Dean Alford says, "The misunderstanding which rendered these words 'within you,' meaning this in a spiritual sense, '*in your hearts*,' should have been prevented by reflecting that they are addressed to the *Pharisees*, in whose hearts it certainly *was not*. We have the very expression, Xen. Anab. 1; 3, *entos autōn*. See also John i, 26, and xii, 35, both of which are analogous expressions." The sentence in which that expression occurs in Xenophon is translated by Charles Anthon, LL.D., Professor of Greek and Latin, thus—"and other things also, as many as were *within their lines* (*entos autōn*) both effects and persons, all they saved." (7). As the Saviour journeyed towards Jerusalem, near the close of his ministry, "they thought that the kingdom of God should immediately appear."—Lu. xix, 11. This proves that it had *not yet* appeared. (8). "I will not drink of the fruit of the vine until the kingdom of God shall come."—Lu. xxii, 18. Thus, "when eating the last supper He distinctly said that the reign of God was then *future*."—A. Campbell, in "Christian System,"

1839, p. 171. Having now brought sufficient proof that the kingdom was not set up before the Saviour's death, let me next invite you to consider,

II. Testimonies proving that it was not set up at Pentecost, and will not be set up before the second coming of Christ. (1). When Peter explained what took place at Pentecost, he did not say, "This is that which was spoken of by the prophet Daniel, *in the days of these kings shall the God of Heaven set up a kingdom*"; but "This is that which was spoken by the prophet Joel, I will pour out my Spirit."—Ac. ii, 16, 17. If the long-predicted kingdom had been set up on that occasion it would certainly have been the *great* event of the day; and it seems to me incredible that the apostles would have neglected to call attention to the fact, especially when I see how prompt they usually were to call attention to less important events that fulfilled some part of prophecy. (2). "We must through much tribulation enter the kingdom of God."—Ac. xiv, 22. This was said about twelve years *after* Pentecost, and proves that the disciples and even Paul himself, though certainly in the church, had *not yet* entered the *kingdom*, but were still waiting for it like the disciples before Pentecost. The tribulation and kingdom are not simultaneous; we must pass "*through*" the former before we enter the latter. The same is taught in 2 Tim. ii, 12; Rom. viii, 17, 18. Paul does not say,

"We *have entered* the kingdom," as many *moderns* tell those who have joined the church. Can you hesitate as to which language is right, Paul's or theirs? It is admitted that he uses a cutting *irony* when (26 years after Pentecost) he says to some, "*Now* ye are full, *now* ye are rich, ye have reigned as *kings* without us. . We are fools for Christ's sake, but ye are wise in Christ; we are weak, but ye are strong." But, dropping the ironical style, he says, " Would to God ye did reign, that *we* also might reign with you."—1 Cor. iv, 8-10. (3). "An entrance *shall be*"—not *has been*—"ministered unto you abundantly into the everlasting kingdom of our Lord and Saviour Jesus Christ." 2 Pet. i, 1, 11. Said about 33 years *after* Pentecost to the church itself, which had "obtained like precious faith" with the apostles. (4). "That ye *may be counted* worthy of the kingdom of God, for which ye also suffer."—2 Thes. i, 5. About 21 years after Pentecost, he does not say, "Ye *have been* counted worthy of the kingdom *in* which ye also suffer." When will they be counted worthy? "When the Son of man shall *come* in His glory" and invite them to "inherit the kingdom."—Mat. xxv, 31, 34. (5), " Walk worthy of God, who is calling you into His kingdom and glory."—1 Thes. 2, 12. This is the correct translation, as given by the American Bible Union. Dean Alford also gives the same rendering, and he remarks, "*Kalountos*, present, because the action is extended on to the future by the following words. God calls us to His *kingdom,* the kingdom of our Lord Jesus, which He shall establish on earth at His coming."

This exhortation of Paul was addressed "to the *church* . . . which is in God the Father, and in the Lord Jesus Christ." See 1 Thes. i, 1. And it shows that God, by spiritual culture and training, is calling the church of the present into the kingdom of the future. This text alone is enough to prove that the church is not the kingdom. It is parallel to 1 Pet. i, 11. The kingdom of God is righteousness, peace, and joy in the Holy Ghost.— Rom. xiv, 17. This appears to be a metonymy in which the effect or end to be obtained is put for the cause that leads to it; as, "I have set before you life and death" (Deut. xxx, 19) i. e. the things which cause or *lead* to life and death. "There is death in the pot" (2 Kin. iv, 40) i. e. a cause leading to death. "To be carnally minded is death." (Rom. viii, 6) i. e. leads to death, as its punishment.* And so righteousness, peace and joy *lead to* an inheritance in the kingdom at last; but a contention with brethren about meats and drinks will not do this, for "meat commended us not to God," and "the *unrighteous* shall *not* inherit the kingdom of God."—1 Cor. vi, 9; viii, 8. (6),

---

* "Instances of metonymy of the effect for the cause, are, in the sacred writings, innumerable."—A. Campbell, in Chr. Res. p. 39, 1839.

"The kingdom which He hath *promised* (it does not say hath *given*) to them that love Him."—Jas. ii, 5. James speaks in the *same* way of the crown of life, which is is also future—" the crown of life which the Lord hath *promised* to them that love Him."—Jas. i, 12. (7). " *Then* shall the righteous shine forth as the sun *in* the kingdom of their Father." This does not occur before the great day of " harvest," as the context plainly shows.—Mat. xiii, 43. (8). He " shall judge the living and the dead at His appearing and His kingdom." So we are not to expect His *kingdom* until His *appearing;* these events God hath joined together, and let not any human creed put them asunder.—2 Tim. iv, 1. (9). The very *same* latter day signs indicate the nearness of the *kingdom* and of our *redemption;* hence the kingdom and the redemption will come simultaneously, for the Lord hath joined them together. (10). " Flesh and blood cannot inherit the kingdom of God."—1 Cor. xv, 50.* That one sentence is enough to prove that Christians are *not yet* in the kingdom. Is it not a very *carnal* view to say that mortal and erring creatures in the present " flesh and blood" nature do enter and commence their reign in that kingdom

---

* "They to whom it is granted to enter into the kingdom of God, will have to put on the power of an incorruptible and immortal life; for without this, before they are able to obtain it, they cannot enter the kingdom of God."—Tertullian (about A.D. 200) De Res. ch. 50.—Clark.

as soon as they join the church? A modern writer who taught that the church is the kingdom, has even said that, "The kingdom which Jesus received from his Father, however heavenly, sublime, and glorious it may be regarded, is only temporal. It had a beginning, and it will have an end."—(Chr. Sys. p. 153, edition 1839). I suppose this was perfectly consistent with the popular modern notion of a present church-kingdom, but it is contrary to Scripture, which plainly declares that "of His kingdom there shall be *no end*," and calls it "the *everlasting* kingdom of our Lord and Saviour Jesus Christ."—Lu. i, 32, 33; 2 Pet. i, 11. (11). The whole structure of the parable of the Pounds proves that the kingdom which the Nobleman went to receive does not appear until He "In bliss returns to *reign*," as the missionary hymn says.—Lu. xix, 12–27.* (12). It is not when they enter the church, but when they rise from the grave that the saints begin their reign with Christ.—Rev. xx, 4. (13). The time for them to possess the *kingdom* does not arrive until the Ancient of days comes, that is, until Christ comes " in the *glory* of

---

* " He went to receive solemn investiture of that kingdom which He had purchased with His blood, and which hereafter He shall return and claim as His own sitting on the throne of His father David."—Trench, Dean of Westminster. "That which they thought should *immediately appear*, Christ tells them will not appear, till this same Jesus, which is taken into heaven, shall in like manner come again; see Ac. i, 11."—HENRY.

His *Father*."—Dan. vii, 22; Mat. xvi, 27. (14). Certainly when the kingdom is set up, Christ, the King, will take His seat on His glorious throne, but He does not take that seat until His *coming;* hence the kingdom is not set up till then.—Mat. xxv, 31. (15). It would be unseemly for the nobles of a kingdom to obtain their coronets and subordinate thrones before the king obtains his; hence the Saviour does not say *before* but "*when* the Son of man shall sit in the throne of His glory, ye (apostles) also shall sit upon twelve thrones." And when will that be? Let His own words be our answer—" When the Son of man shall COME in His glory and all the holy angels with Him, THEN shall he sit upon the throne of His glory."—Mat. xix, 28, with xxv, 31. (16). When the kingdom is set up the descending Stone is to smite the image in its *divided* state i. e. on its feet and toes of iron and clay. But at the *first* advent the image had not arrived at its divided state but was existing in its *iron* form and under *one* head, as proved by the decree from its *one* ruler at Rome "that all the world should be taxed." Hence the smiting which attends the setting up of the kingdom did not take place at the first advent. The image did not commence being divided into the ten parts, indicated by the ten toes, until the fourth century after the first advent.—Dan. ii, 34, 44; Lu. ii, 1. Plainly enough prophecy shows that the image is to be smitten in the days, not of iron *only*, as at the first advent, but in the days of "*iron and clay.*"—Dan. ii, 34, 42. Nor does the stone go softly up to the image and gradually absorb it as by the mild and gentle wooings of the gospel, but suddenly smites it with a *crushing* blow (Mat. xxi, 44), and "THEN" the fragments are swept away so that no place is found for them; verse 35. Think you that we should find human governments in the world to-day, if that smiting had occurred eighteen hundred years ago ? *

Having clearly proved that the kingdom is not to be set up until the second advent, let me now call your attention to some of the signs which denote that it is "nigh at hand." We are not to neglect this branch of study, but are commanded to give attention to the signs and learn the lesson which they teach. "When ye see these things come to pass, *know ye* that the kingdom of God is

---

* The celebrated commentary of Jamieson, Faussett and Brown says. on Dan. ii, "The kingdom of God coming from heaven originally, ends in heaven being established on earth. . . 'In the days of these kings' answers to 'upon his feet' (v. 34) i. e. 'the ten toes' (v. 42), or ten kings, the final state of the Roman empire. The falling of the stone on the image must mean *destroying judgment* on the fourth Gentile power, not gradual evangelization of it by grace; and the destroying judgment cannot be dealt by christians, for they are taught to submit to the powers that be, so that it must be dealt by Christ himself at His coming again. We live under the divisions of the Roman empire which began 1400 years ago, and which at the time of His coming shall be definitely ten."

nigh at hand."—Lu. xxi, 31. "Can ye not discern the signs of the times?"—Mat. xvi, 3. By the chart of prophecy we can discover very nearly at what point in this world's career the church has now arrived. Daniel, in his interpretation of the great image and of the four beasts (chapters ii and vii) has delineated with wonderful clearness the course of events from his own time until the second advent. Here is a very ancient and admirable summary of those two visions, given by Hippolytus, who was martyred A.D. 235, and who is pronounced by the "Comprehensive Commentary" to be "one of the most distinguished of the ancient fathers and martyrs." He says:—"The golden head of the image, and the lioness, denoted the Babylonians; the shoulders and arms of silver, and the bear, represented the Persians and Medes; the belly and thighs of brass, and the leopard, meant the Greeks, who held the sovereignty from Alexander's time; the legs of iron, and the beast dreadful and terrible, expressed the Romans, who hold the sovereignty at present; the toes of the feet, which were part clay and part iron, and the ten horns, were emblems of the kingdoms that are yet to rise; the other little horn that grows up among them meant the Anti-Christ in their midst; the stone that smites the earth and brings judgment upon the world was Christ. . . After a little space the Stone *will come* from heaven which smites the image and breaks it in pieces, and subverts all the kingdoms, and gives the kingdom to the saints of the Most High. This is the Stone which becomes a great mountain and fills the whole earth."—Treatise on Christ and Antichrist, 26, 28, Clark's ed., Edinburgh.

Hippolytus wrote *before* the division of the empire, and see how wonderfully history has verified his view of the prophecy! Observe, too, that he did not fall into the modern error of supposing the Stone had smitten the image at the *first* advent. For greater clearness let me present the visions of Dan. ii and vii in the following parallel form, the left column being the four metals of the image, and the right the four beasts. Some things are represented by the beasts which could not be represented by the metals; hence the one set of symbols is supplemented by the other.

The fourth, like the three that went before it, was to be a great *predominating* human empire, as indicated by the saying that it should " devour the *whole earth,* and tread it down, and break it in pieces."—Dan. vii, 23. That the *Roman* was that fourth great empire is proved by its closely succeeding the third, and having authority to send out a decree from Rome " that *all the world* should be taxed."—Lu. ii, 1. Notice how beautifully the Bible is its own interpreter in all this great succession of empires, telling us which would succeed which, and that the glorious and eternal KINGDOM OF GOD shall succeed them all.

(Dan. ii.)

THE GOLD.

Babylonian empire, ruling "wheresoever the children of men dwell."—ver. 38. Overthrown and succeeded by the Medo-Persian, about 538 B. C.—Dan. v, 28, 31.

THE SILVER.

Medo-Persian empire, under Cyrus, who declared "All the kingdoms of the earth" were given him.—Ezra i, 2. Succeeded about 330 B. C. by the Grecian. In Dan. viii, 5, 7, 20, 21, this is represented by an he-goat conquering a ram.

THE BRASS.

Grecian empire, bearing "rule over all the earth," ver. 39. "The brazen-coated Greeks." After Alexander's death it was divided into 4 kingdoms and finally succeeded by the Roman empire, which arrived at the meridian of its power about 19 B. C.

THE IRON.

First phase: The unmixed iron was the Roman empire in its undivided state. Second phase: The "iron mixed with *clay*" is the same empire after it became divided, first into Eastern and Western, and afterwards into 10 kingdoms. The first clang of the descending Stone is not on the silver, gold, brass or iron, but on the *iron and clay* (v, 34, 41), *then* the rest are pulverized and the KINGDOM OF GOD fills the earth.—ver. 35, 44.

(Dan. vii.)

THE LION

Answers to the gold of the image. A winged lion denoted strength and swiftness in war. But was humbled by defeat—"a man's heart was given it."—ver. 4; Psa. ix, 20.

THE BEAR

Answers to the silver breast and arms—the Medes and Persians united in one empire. A bear indicates their bloodthirsty cruelty. Isa. xiii, 18. Three ribs probably denote the "three presidents."—Dan. vi, 2.

THE LEOPARD

Answers to the brass. With 4 wings, denoted the daring and impetuosity of Alexander and his army. Four heads represent the 4 kingdoms into which the empire was divided after Alexander's death.—Dan. viii, 8, 22; xi, 4.

THE FOURTH BEAST

Answers to the iron and iron mixed with clay. It succeeds the leopard as the iron did the brass. Its two rows of "great *iron* teeth" (vii, 7) answer to the two legs of iron; its 10 horns to the 10 toes of the image. The Lamb overcoming the 10 kings and other foes at the advent, and His subsequent reign with the risen saints answers to crushing the toes, &c., and the setting up of the KINGDOM OF GOD.—See Rev. xvii, 14· xix, 19; xx, 4.

These visions of Daniel describe the course of events from his time until the setting up of the kingdom of God. The human kingdoms all "arise out of the earth," not one of them forming any part of that image is said to be "of heaven." Hence they are fitly represented by metals dug out of the earth, and by fierce wild beasts coming "out of the sea," whose troubled waters "casting up mire and dirt" are emblematic of the wicked. Daniel vii, 3, 17 ; Isa. lvii, 20. Well, taking the Bible in one hand and history in the other, we find in the preceding chart, by the severely accurate logic of historical events, that we are now living in the very last extremity of the image, in the very last days of mortal rule, and on the verge of the moment when the descending Stone will crush into dust all human governments and fill the earth with the kingdom of God. When Paul wrote to the Thessalonians he certainly did not place the advent in an indefinite future, but plainly taught that *some* generation of believers— those who "are alive and remain"—shall be eye-witnesses of the advent, and that it should occur after a certain power then existing should be taken out of the way, and the man of sin developed.—1 Thes. iv, 16, 17 ; 2 Thes. ii, 8 *

---

* Instead of "is at hand," in verse 2, read "is come" or "is present," for so the Greek signifies. To think the day had already *come* and not brought the Lord with it was enough to *trouble* them and to *shake* their faith (see 2 Tim.

But signs even more vivid than those already considered are given for the comfort and warning of waiting and watching ones, by which they may know that "the morning cometh and also the night"—the morning of endless joy for the righteous, the night of eternal death for the wicked,—Isa. xxi, 12. The constant drying up or wasting away of the power symbolized by the "great river Euphrates" is one of those signs. See Rev. xvi, 12-15. Anciently the Assyrian empire, bordering on that river, was the political Euphrates, and that nation, extending itself and conquering its neighbors, was compared to that river overflowing its banks.—Isa. viii, 7. Hence the wasting away of that empire or nation might have been aptly compared to the drying up of that river. There can hardly be a doubt but that, in symbolic language, the *Turks* are the *modern* Euphrates. (Waters, in the very next chapter, "are peoples and multitudes and nations and tongues."- Rev. xvii, 15.) I think we first get a view of that nation under the 6th Trumpet, when the four angels, or four sultanies of the Turks, were loosed from the great river Euphrates as a warlike scourge

ii, 18); but why should they be "troubled" at the joyful tidings that the day is near? "The teaching of the apostles was, and of the Holy Spirit in all ages has been, that the day of the Lord *is at hand*. But these Thessalonians imagined it to be *already come*, and accordingly were deserting their pursuits in life, and falling into other irregularities, as if the day of grace were closed."—ALFORD.

upon the nations west of that river. On that loosing of the four angels the "Comprehensive Commentary" says:—"This is explained by the most approved interpreters, according to the emblematical style of the prophecy, to be a prediction that the TURKS, or OTHMANS, who had hitherto been restrained beyond the EUPHRATES, would be released from that restraint, and proceed to make conquests to the west of that river." And thus I think we may regard the 6th *Trumpet* as a *key* by which to interpret the 6th *Vial*. A glance at the history of the Turkish Empire from A.D. 1820 to the present time will show how steadily has been progressing the drying up of that fearful Euphratean inundation, which once carried consternation into Europe itself. In addition to wasting and amputating wars, the empire has been internally weakened by revolts, massacres, plagues, conflagrations, and general mismanagement. Taking a mere dull and secular view of the facts, Alison, as an historian, testifies that "generally speaking, the country is retrograde, and exhibits the usual and well-known features of decaying societies." Fleming, an old writer on prophecy, considered "that, as the 6th Trumpet (Rev. ix, 13–19) brought the Turks from beyond the Euphrates, so the 6th Vial exhausts their power." But why call this drying up a sign of the advent? Because it is announced under the *same* vial (the 6th) with the announcement of the Lord's coming.

Martin Luther, long ago (he died in 1546) had the wisdom to perceive this, for he says, " When the Turk begins to decline, then the last day will be at hand, for the testimony of the Scripture must be verified."—In his "Table Talk," of the resurrection. Translated by Hazlitt.

The rapid decline of "the sick man," as the Turk has been called, brings England upon the scene to look after her interests in his estate. And this becomes on the prophetic horizon another bright streak of the coming dawn for it leads us to hope for a great improvement of Palestine and for a speedy gathering there of the number of Jews which prophecy requires to be in the land at the Lord's coming. There must be some such gathering there for when Gog marches against them "*in the latter days*" they are described as "the people that are gathered out of the nations, which have gotten cattle and goods."—Eze. xxxviii, 12–16. That however is not the great restoration of Israel but only as the few large drops that precede the shower. The required number of settlers may soon be obtained. Already towards that land a tide seems to have set in of returning Israelites.

And simultaneously with the decline of Turkey is the aggrandisement of Russia, and her encroachment upon the Turk. This too is a sign, for prophecy requires that " in the latter days " a vast military host shall come " out of the *north* parts " with many allied bands " against the mountains of

Israel," and the Jews gathered there; but that host shall then perish at the "*presence*" of the Lord, which indicates that He will *come* at *that time*.—Eze. xxxviii, 15–23. On this and the succeeding chapter of Ezekiel the Comprehensive Commentary says, "If any part of the ancient prophecies allude more plainly than others to *the latter days*, it is this of Ezekiel concerning Gog and Magog. It has undoubtedly not received its completion." But why suppose that "Gog, the land of Magog, the chief prince of Meshech and Tubal" means Russia? Because history and geography point that way. They dwell in "the *north* parts" ("*the uttermost north*,"— Septuagint). Eze. xxxviii, 15, and xxxix, 2. Maury's Intermediate Geography, 1876, says, Russia has been called "The Colossus of the North," on account of its great size and strength. It is the northernmost great empire on the globe. Daniel, speaking as I believe of the same invasion, calls its commander "the King of the north," and tells of his destruction at the resurrection, that is, at the *advent*, for the resurrection will not occur *before* the Lord comes.—Dan. xi, 40, 45, and xii, 2. Watson's Theol. Dict. says, "Gog and Magog, the general name of the northern nations of Europe and Asia, or the districts north of the Caucassus or mount Taurus." In a foot note on Gen. x, 2, (1873) The American Bible Union says that instead of "the chief prince of Meshech and Tubal," in Eze. xxxviii, 2, it ought to be translated, "the prince of Rosh, Meshech and Tubal.'" It then adds, "*Rosh* (according to the best authorities) is identical with *Rus* and *Russia*, and is the earliest trace of that powerful people. The obliteration of it, by the authorized version, is one of the many remarkable variations of our version from the meaning of the sacred text of the Old Testament." The Septuagint also has "*Rosh*" here, which in Greek becomes "*Rōs.*"

Now when Russia and her allied nations invade the land of Israel they will find themselves confronted by foes called "Sheba and Dedan, and the merchants of Tarshish with all the young lions thereof."—Eze. xxxviii, 8–13. As to the location of "*Tarshish*" there were anciently, it seems, two countries of that name, Eastern and Western, somewhat as now there are E. and W. Indies. At Ezion-gaber, a port on the Red Sea, were built "ships to go to Tarshish"; and once in three years they brought "gold, silver, ivory, apes and peacocks"—products now found in *India;* and so perhaps this was the eastern Tarshish.—2 Chron. ix, 21, and xx, 36; 1 Kin. x, 22. Also we find that from Joppa, now Jaffa on the Mediterranean, Jonah embarked on "a ship going to Tarshish." This would seem to point out a Western Tarshish from which Tyre, a Phœnician city, obtained "silver, iron, *tin* and lead."—Eze. xxvii, 12. Fitch's "Physical Geography" says, "The most productive *tin* mining region in the world is Cornwall, England. The Cornish mines have been worked from a very early period, the metal from which formed an article of *traffic with the Phœnicians* and Greeks before the time of our Saviour." This prophecy therefore seems to point to the *British* forces and their allies assembled about Palestine to defend the British route to India; and indeed to defend India itself; for it seems probable that the snatching of India from England will be one of the motives with which Russia will invade the land of Israel. These military movements will produce a vast confluence of peoples to Palestine. One of the effects of the sixth vial, besides drying up the Euphrates, is to gather "the kings of the earth and of the whole world" to a great assemblage in "a place called in the Hebrew tongue *Armageddon*"—the name being in the Hebrew tongue indicates the place to be in the Hebrew *land* i. e. Palestine. Closely connected with this gathering is the announcement, "*Behold I come* as a thief, blessed is he that watcheth and keepeth his garments."—Rev. xvi, 12–15.

The intricacies of human policy are often overruled by Him who maketh the wrath of man praise Him, and so the movements of the Russians, the Turks, the Jews and the British, appear to be one grand system of signs, all converging to the formation of that crisis in Palestine which will bring the Lord Jesus personally upon the scene.

We live in an age of rapid movements, and the *advent* crisis may be quickly formed. It will be sure to take the great stupid, sleepy, surfeiting, avaricious and wicked world entirely by surprise. 1 Thes. v, 3, 4. But O, how ardently does the Christian yearn for that event! and his fervent prayer is, "Come, Lord Jesus, come quickly." "Wherefore, beloved, seeing that ye look for such things, be diligent that ye may be found of Him in peace, without spot and blameless."—2 Pet. iii, 14. Are you living still a worldling and without hope? I beseech you to become a Christian without delay, lest you soon find repentance to be *too late*, and, like those in the parable, cry out "Lord, Lord, open unto us," after the door of mercy has been closed. That was a good prayer, and earnest enough, no doubt, but it was *too late*.

> "Procrastination is the thief of time;
> Year after year it steals, till *all* are fled,
> And to the *mercies of a moment* leaves
> The vast concerns of an *eternal* scene.
> If not so frequent, would not this be strange?
> That 'tis so frequent, this is stranger still."

Too late is one of the most common causes of failure in life. One is too late to secure an education which was neglected in youth, and finds himself in riper age pressed by cares which prevent him from gathering up the lost opportunities. Another is too late to restore a constitution shattered by excess, and broods in despair over the folly that refused to be warned in time. A merchant is too late to avert a failure in business, and so the toil of years is lost by some calamity which a little timely precaution might have prevented. A patient dies because the physician is too late in coming to see him. I've read of a physician who committed suicide for a fault of this kind. Many have to lament concerning some dear one beneath the sod, "Oh! if I had known sooner of such and such a remedy; but now it is too late."

Some of these mistakes, however, can be remedied in some degree; but to be too late in securing salvation is to be too late *forever*. "Because I called and ye refused... I also will laugh at your calamity, I will mock when your fear cometh."—Prov. i, 24, 26. For a long time your sins have provoked the Lord, and He has endured it—"These things hast thou done, and I kept *silence*"; but the time is hastening when "Our God shall *come* and shall *not* keep silence; a fire shall devour before Him, and it shall be very tempestuous round about Him."—Psa. L, 3, 21. There is to be a fearful punishment for the wicked when the Lord comes, and is it wise to act as though indolence, thoughtlessness or neglect will save you from it? As well suppose that shutting your eyes would protect you from the rage of a devouring lion, or that looking another way would prevent your body from being pierced by a bullet or a sword. What is to be gained by delaying to become a Christian? Will you become better by delay? Evil men "wax worse and worse." Will your heart become more tender by long continuance in sin? Beware lest you become so "*accustomed* to do evil" that your conscience become seared, and you find it as hard to do well as an Ethiopian to change his skin or a leopard his spots. Will the gospel ever be more powerful, Christ's blood more efficacious, or God's love any freer than *now?* Or will delay enable you at the hour of death to look upon a greater number of years devoted to the service of God? You ought to want to give a *long* time to His service, and yet every moment that you lose in delaying to become a Christian brings you nearer the grave and shortens the time that you might spend in serving the Lord. Have you been anxious and distressed about your salvation, forgetting even to eat the victuals placed on your plate, or mingling every mouthful with your tears? Come to Jesus; believe the gospel of the kingdom; arise and be baptized and wash away thy sins. Thus you will be "a *new* creature," and the Saviour will extend to you peace like a flowing stream, even that heavenly peace which the world cannot give and cannot take away.

Do not put off baptism until warmer weather; you cannot put off *death* in that way. Do you hesitate because baptism seems a slight inconvenience to the flesh? It can be nothing to compare with what the Saviour endured *for you*, when, surrounded by scoffing enemies, He expired, all pierced and bleeding, on the cross.

[From "Songs of Zion."]

How blest are all that hither come;
   And mindful of His word,
Are planted in the wat'ry tomb:
   For so was Christ the Lord.

Then rising from the cleansing wave,
   A holy life to lead,
They will His aid and comfort have
   In ev'ry time of need.

For scenes like this there's joy among
   The Angels bright above;
And on the earth, in sacred song,
   We praise redeeming love.

TENTH DISCOURSE.

THE SECOND ADVENT, THE MILLENNIUM, AND THE STATE BEYOND.

"They lived and reigned with Christ a thousand years."—
REV. xx; 4.

That the Lord Jesus will personally and visibly come to this earth again is a truth so generally admitted that but little argument is needed on the subject. I will, however, quote a few testimonies in proof of it. Predictions of His two comings run like two golden threads throughout the Old Testament—the first as an humble Sufferer, the next as a royal Conquerer. Hence Peter says the prophets "testified beforehand the *sufferings* of Christ, and the *glories* following these," *tas meta tauta doxas.*—1 Pet. i, 11. The first promise of redemption implies both comings—the first, at which the serpent was to bruise his heel; the second, at which He will bruise or crush the serpent's head.—Gen. iii, 15. Enoch, the seventh from Adam, prophesied, "Behold, the Lord cometh with ten thousand of His saints"; and Jude refers this prophecy to the *future judgment.* Jude 14. Job says, "He shall stand at the latter day *upon the earth;* and though *after* my skin worms destroy this body, yet in my *flesh* shall I see God."—Job xix, 25–27. The margin says, "After I shall *awake,*" i. e. by a *resurrection*, as the word is used elsewhere, "Many that sleep in the dust of the earth shall *awake.*"—Dan. xii, 2. "I go that I may *awake* him."—John xi, 11. When can that standing *upon the earth* be except at the *resurrection*, when "the Lord *himself* shall descend from heaven and the dead in Christ shall rise"?—1 Thes. iv, 16, 17. "Our God shall *come,* and shall not keep silence; a *fire* shall devour before Him, and it shall be very tempestuous round about Him. . . Gather my saints together *unto* me."—Psa. L, 3, 4. Paul evidently refers to the same event as "the *coming* of our Lord Jesus Christ, in flaming *fire*, and our *gathering* together *unto Him*."—2 Thes. i, 7, 8; ii, 1. "And His feet shall stand in that day upon the *mount of Olives*, which is before Jerusalem on the east."—Zec. xiv, 4, 5. "The place of His throne, and the place of the soles of His feet" will be in the New Jerusalem on earth.—Eze. xliii, 7; Rev. xxii, 3. Two trees, when some distance off in front of you, if viewed nearly on a line with each other, will not seem so far apart as they really are. But on placing yourself .between them you see the real distance. So we are now living *between* the advents, looking back on the one and forward to the other. But the prophets who lived before *both* advents often delineated them somewhat perspectively, and nearly in the same breath, without describing the long interval between; so that, to the careless reader, events belonging to the first advent seem almost to blend with events belonging to the second.—See Isa. ix, 6, 7; Zec. ix, 9, 10; Mic. v, 2.

Turning now to the New Testament, His advent as a sufferer becomes a matter of *history*, while His future advent as a royal Conquerer still remains a prediction, and is foretold in clear and glowing language. "They shall *see* the Son of Man coming in the clouds of heaven with *power* and *great glory*."—Mat. xxiv, 30. "The bridegroom *came*, and they that were ready went in with him to the marriage." "After a long time the Lord of those servants *cometh*, and reckoneth with them."—Mat. xxv, 10, 19. "When he was *returned*, having received the kingdom, he commanded those servants to be called."—Lu. xix, 15. In these three parables, if the going away was literal so must the return be. And this reminds us of the testimony given when He literally and visibly ascended from the *mount of Olives*—"This *same* Jesus which is taken up from you into heaven shall *so come in like manner* as ye have *seen* him *go* into heaven."—Ac. i, 11. Surely this ought to be an end of controversy on the subject. If He ascended visibly and personally, he must come visibly and personally. And with wonderful harmony this prophecy of the two white-robed messengers agrees with that in Zechariah xiv, 4, which declares that "His feet shall stand in that day upon the *mount of Olives*, which is before Jerusalem on the east." This is the identical mountain from which He ascended. I once heard that some preacher said, "It would be egregious nonsense to say that the Lord Jesus will ever come to this cursed earth again." I dislike to repeat such language, except to show how entirely opposed it is to the Bible; for, after the testimonies already produced, we see that it would be egregious nonsense to say that He will *not* come to this earth again. Would that the whole of the Episcopal creed were as true as the 4th article, which says, "Christ did truly rise again from death, and took again His *body*, with *flesh, bones*, and all things appertaining to the perfection of man's nature, *wherewith* He ascended into heaven, and there sitteth, until He *return* to judge all men at the last day." This is not mortal and corruptible but immortal and incorruptible "flesh and bones."—Lu. xxiv, 39. It does not read "flesh and blood," for Spirit becomes the vitalizing element in the bodies of the risen saints, which will be "fashioned like unto" that of their Lord.—Phil. iii, 21. Such a body will have "flesh and bones, and all things appertaining to the *perfection*," but nothing to the *imperfections* of man's nature.

The fact that the Lord's Supper is still an ordinance of the church is proof that the Lord has not yet come "a second time," for "as oft as ye eat this bread, and drink this cup, ye do show the Lord's death *till He come*."—1 Cor. xi, 26; Heb. ix, 28. Hence the constant attitude of the Christian is that of "looking for" and "waiting for" His return, nor can any but those who "*love* His appearing" have a well-grounded hope of obtaining the "crown of righteousness."—Heb. ix, 28; 1 Thes. i, 10; 2 Tim. iv, 8. Death is not the Lord's coming, for when the early Christians talked of one's tarrying "till He come," they meant that such an one should *not* die.—John xxi, 22, 23. And they were perfectly right in this, for Paul himself repeatedly taught it—" We shall not *all* sleep," but some will be " *alive* and *remain* unto the coming of the Lord," and these, together with the risen saints, will be caught away to meet the Lord.—1 Cor. xv, 51; 1 Thes. iv, 15, 16, 17. Thus believers who are then dead shall live, and those who are then alive " shall never die."—John xi, 26. Death is near, but the Lord's coming may be *nearer*. Let one more quotation suffice to prove the Lord's literal and personal coming—" The Lord *himself* shall descend from heaven with a shout, with the voice of the Archangel, and with the trump of God; and the dead in Christ shall rise first; then we which are alive and remain shall be caught up together with them in the clouds, to meet the Lord."—1 Thes. iv, 16, 17 * Here is the personal descent of the Lord *himself*, and the righteous dead are personally and literally raised, and, together with those who are personally and literally alive and remain, they are caught away to meet the Lord. This is a personal meeting, a personal resurrection and a personal descent of the Lord; and it would be wickedly torturing Scripture to try to give it a mystified or figurative meaning. The mere expression " to meet," *eis*

---

* "So far were the early Christians from regarding their departed brethren as *anticipating* them in entering glory, that they needed to be assured that those who remain to the coming of the Lord will not anticipate them that are asleep." —*Commentary of Jamieson, Faussett & Brown.*

apantēsin, proves it personal, for that is its meaning in its three other occurrences in the New Testament.—Mat. xxvi, 1, 6; Ac. xxviii, 15.

That the Millennium (the period of one thousand years mentioned six times in Rev. xx) does not commence until *after* the Lord Jesus comes, is evident from the following reasons :—

1st. During the *entire* absence of the Bridegroom the Church is represented as in a *mourning* and *fasting* state that does not accord with millennial prosperity and glory. " Jesus said unto them, Can the children of the bride-chamber *mourn* as long as the Bridegroom is *with* them? but the days will come when the Bridegroom shall be *taken from* them, and *then* shall they fast."—Mat. ix, 15. At the *return* of the Bridegroom, however, the great command goes forth, " Let us *be glad* and *rejoice,* and give honor to Him ; for the *marriage* of the Lamb is come, and His wife hath made herself ready."—Rev. xix, 7. The parable of the ten virgins proves that return to be *personal;* hence the mourning and fasting period extends to the personal advent, instead of ending a thousand years *before* it.—Mat. xxv, 1–10. This argument alone is enough to prove that we can have no millennial glory so long as the Bridegroom is away; but the glorious Millennium will most appropriately *follow* His return.

2nd. And, most plainly, as the coming of the heavenly Bridegroom does not find the Church in a millennial but a mourning state, so neither does it find the world in a millennial state, but as it was in the days of Noah (i. e. "filled with *violence*" instead of "knowledge of the Lord."—Gen. vi, 13; Isa. xi, 9). It will be like Sodom and Gomorrha. The wheat and tares will be growing together, and scarcely any of "*the* faith on the earth."—Lu. xvii, 26–30; xviii, 8; Mat. xiii, 30. The Greek definite article here refers to the *true* faith. No doubt He will find much false or unscriptural faith, for that abounds. After such plain declarations as this, how can *any* one doubt the premillennial advent?

3rd. The Scripture has *not* said that the gospel would *convert* all nations among whom it was preached, but the *purpose* of God in sending it to them was "to take *out of them* a people for His name." Hence we are not to expect the conversion of all nations under the gospel dispensation.—Ac. xv, 14.

4th. If the gospel of the kingdom, when carried into all the world by the apostles, did not millennialize even *one* nation, though aided by the *gift of tongues* and *working of miracles*, how can it hereafter be expected to millennialize *all* nations *without* those aids? It is when the *judgments* of the Lord are "made manifest" by the conquering power of the returned Messiah, that the remnant of the inhabitants of the world "will learn righteousness," after vast numbers of them shall have been destroyed.—Rev. xv, 4; Isa. xxvi, 9 ; Psa. lviii, 10, 11 ; Zec. xiv, 16. The kingdom to be established in the covenanted land, though like a mustard-seed or leaven at first, will quickly grow and spread by *miraculous conquest,* and " fill the whole earth."

5th. " The whole world lieth in wickedness," and " all that will live godly in Christ Jesus shall suffer persecution."—1 Jno. v, 19 ; 2 Tim. iii, 12. This is perfectly appropriate to a sinning world and a suffering church ; and no doubt it will be appropriate until the Saviour comes. But would it be at all applicable to a millennial dispensation when Satan is *bound,* the world *converted,* and persecution has *ceased?*

6th. The blessed Saviour, in giving an outline of events from His first until His second coming, has described a long period of tribulations and wrath upon the Jews, and also the downtreading of Jerusalem " until the times of the Gentiles be fulfilled." Now it must be admitted that the joyful millennium will not commence until that tribulation ends. And yet it is " IMMEDIATELY," and not a thousand years, after that tribulation ends that the signs of the *second advent* are seen. Hence there is *no room* for the Millennium between the advent and the tribulation ; the advent must therefore be *pre*-millennial. To obtain a clear view of the prophecy in a few words, read it in this order—" There shall be *great distress* in the land and *wrath* upon *this people.* And they shall fall by the edge of the sword, and shall be led away captive into all nations; and Jerusalem shall be trodden down of the Gentiles *until* the times of the Gentiles be fulfillled (Lu. xxi, 23, 24). Immediately *after* the tribulation of those days shall the sun be darkened, and the moon shall not give her light, and the stars shall fall from heaven, and the powers of the heavens shall be shaken; and *then* shall appear the sign of the Son of man in heaven; and then shall all the tribes of the earth *mourn,* and they shall *see* the Son of man *coming* in the clouds of heaven with power and great glory."—Matt. xxiv, 29, 30.*

7th. And as the Saviour did not predict a Millennium of rest and triumph between the first and second advent, neither did Paul predict such a season as obtaining before the advent, but rather a great *apostasy* from the faith, which would last until the Lord's coming.—2 Thes. ii, 1–8. The word coming in v. 8 is *parousia* the *same* word that in v. 1 is translated "coming;" which coming (in v. 1) the "Comprehensive Commentary" says, "All the best commentators, ancient and modern, understand of Christ's second advent." It must

---

* "The important insertion of ver. 23, 24 in Luke shows us that the *tribulation* includes *wrath on this people* which *is yet being inflicted,* and the treading down of Jerusalem by the Gentiles still going on."—ALFORD.

therefore mean the same in v. 8 where it is combined with another word which also signifies a personal appearing. That word is *epiphaneia*, here rendered " brightness," but in its five other occurrences it is translated " appearing."—1 Tim. vi, 4; 2 Tim. i 10, and iv, i, 8; Titus ii, 13. *Parousia* also means a *personal* coming, as " the coming (*parousia*) of Stephanas, Fortunatus," &c., who brought substantial help to Paul.—1 Cor. xvi, 17. Either of these words is held sufficient in other passages to prove a real and personal appearing and presence. And when both are *united* as in the case before us, how is it possible that they should mean anything less than the literal, real and personal arrival and presence of the Lord Jesus? Thus we find no room for a millennium between Paul's day and the personal advent, but the mystery of iniquity which did already work was to continue its desolating career until destroyed at the Lord's coming.

8th. So also in John's prophecy. The Bible does not speak of an *eighth* trumpet. Hence I conclude that the seventh trumpet of which John speaks is " the *last* trumpet " at which time Paul says "the Lord *himself* shall descend from heaven," and the dead in Christ arise.—1 Cor. xv, 52, with 1 Thes. iv, 16. John places the resurrection, &c., under the *seventh* trumpet which, I think, sufficiently identifies it with the last trumpet of Paul.—Rev. xi, 15–18. Now the argument is this, that, up to the sounding of the seventh trumpet is a scene of *wars, commotions, persecutions,* and *sufferings,* with no room nor interspace for thrusting in edgewise a thousand years of peace and prosperity; and the seventh trumpet itself is "the third *woe.*"— Rev. xi, 14. Hence that period must come *after* the seventh trumpet, and therefore after the *advent and resurrection.* Now if it would be absurd to say that the seventh trumpet is not sounded until the end of the millennium, would it not be equally so to say that the advent does not occur till the end of the millennium? I think this argument alone concerning the seventh trumpet is enough to prove the advent *pre-*millennial. Here is how the "Comprehensive Commentary" describes the arrangement of the seals, trumpets and vials, (an arrangement followed very closely, I believe, by the best modern writers on the Apocalypse, from Vitringa of the 17th to Dr. Thomas of the 19th century)—"Fraser thus expresses the arrangement recommended by Vitringa, and now *generally adopted.* The series of events is carried on in the Apocalypse, by seven seals opened in their order, seven trumpets sounded in their order, and seven vials poured out in their order. The seven trumpets are the evolution of the seventh seal, the seven vials are the evolution of the seventh trumpet. The seventh vial introduces the Millennium."— Vol. v.

Let me call your attention to this chart which

THE SEVEN SEALS.		THE MILLENNIUM.
1, 2, 3, 4, 5, 6,	7.	
	THE SEVEN TRUMPETS.	
	1, 2, 3, 4, 5, 6, 7.	
	The 7 Vials.	
	1, 2, 3, 4, 5, 6, 7.	

I have drawn up to show the beautiful and systematic manner in which the seals, trumpets and vials are planned. You perceive that the seven trumpets fall under the seventh seal as so many parts or subdivisions of that seal, and the seven vials fall under the seventh trumpet as so many parts or subdivisions of that trumpet. The six seals, like so many chapters of history, are supposed to extend from about A.D. 98 to the overthrow of the Pagan Roman empire, about A.D. 324. Then the seventh seal, containing the seven trumpets, is said to begin, and to extend to the Millennium. The six trumpets, like so many chapters under that seal, are supposed to extend to the French revolution, about A.D. 1789. Then the seventh trumpet, containing the seven vials, is said to begin its course (called "the days of the voice of the seventh angel," Rev. x, 7.) and extend to the Millennium. The seven vials, like seven chapters of the world's history are thought to commence about A.D. 1789 and run on till the *sixth*, under which is made the startling announcement of the *advent* (and hence of the *resurrection* also) in these words, "BEHOLD I COME AS A THIEF, BLESSED IS HE THAT WATCHETH AND KEEPETH HIS GARMENTS."—Rev. xvi, 12–15.

After the advent the saints, immortalized then, unite with Christ in executing the seventh vial upon the wicked inhabitants of the earth. Being then invested with the promised "power over the nations" (Rev. ii, 26, 27), they will attend the Messiah as His "called, and chosen, and faithful" ones when He marches forth to His miraculous conquest of the world.—Rev. xvii, 14; xix, 14. "To execute vengeance upon the heathen, and punishment upon the people; to bind their kings with chains, and their nobles with fetters of iron; to execute upon them the *judgment* written: *this honour* have *all* His saints."—Psa. cxlix, 7–9. Kings must always conquer a hostile country before they can reign over it; and so that fearful period of conquest, rapid and miraculous, will precede the blessed and peaceful millennial reign. Thus we find no room in John's prophecy for a thousand years of peace and triumph *before* the Lord's coming.

9th. Daniel describes four great empires closely succeeding one another, and rooted in the head of the fourth is a little horn, or persecuting power, that "makes war with the saints and prevails against them *until* the Ancient of days *comes*."—

Dan. vii, 19–22. He does not say "until a thousand years *before* the Ancient of days comes." Of course the little horn will have to cease making war with the saints and prevailing against them before the Millennium can begin; but it does not cease before Christ comes, who, I suppose, is here called the Ancient of days because "His goings forth have been from of *old*," and He will come clothed "in the *glory* of His *Father*."—Mic. v, 2; Mat. xxv, 31. In the same manner Paul too has put the destruction of the persecuting power at the *coming* of the Lord.—2 Thes. ii, 8. Thus I find neither in the prophecy of Daniel nor Paul any space or room for the Millennium *before* the advent.

10th. If you will study the 14th chapter of Zechariah I think that you will find that chapter to be an invulnerable fortress of proof that the Lord Jesus will come *before* the Millennium.* Verses 4 and 5 plainly describe the second advent, in saying, "*The Lord my God shall* COME, *and all the saints with thee*." Notice too the marginal references on that sentence: in my Bible they are Mat. xvi, 27; xxiv, 30, 31; xxv, 31; Jude 14. All these references relate to the second coming. The

---

* The American Tract Society's Notes here say, "This chapter describes the last great conflict of God's church with her enemies." There will, however, be a *later* conflict —that which occurs at the *end* of the Millennium.—Rev. xx, 9.

first (Mat. xvi, 27) shows it to be the time of *rewarding* the righteous, and this identifies it with the seventh trumpet period, in Rev. xi, 15–18. Then, after describing several wonderful changes in the mount of Olives and adjacent country which have never *yet* occurred, and the mere naming of which proves that the prophet is not referring to any *past* coming, he proceeds in verses 12–15 to describe the great overthow of wicked persons that will occur in the vicinity of Jerusalem at the advent. Neither does history record any such overthrow as this at any time in the past; it must be *future*. And then, AFTER the advent and AFTER that conquest of nations, the prophet goes on in verses 16–21 to describe *the glorious millennial age of peace and blessedness* when the "left" or spared remnant of the nations shall flock to Jerusalem "from year to year to worship the King, the Lord of hosts, and to keep the feast of tabernacles." This implies the deliverance of Jerusalem and the establishment of the kingdom of God over the entire earth, two events which the prophet had merely glanced at in verses 9 and 11.

Absurdly enough some have imagined that the gathering of "*all* nations against Jerusalem, verse 2, was fulfilled at the *Roman* invasion. But this is only a *partial* captivity, for "HALF of the city shall go forth into captivity, and the residue of the people shall NOT be cut off from the city." The Roman invasion does not at all agree with this, for then the *whole* city was destroyed, nor was the Roman nation *all* nations. Josephus says, "As soon as the army had *no more people* to slay, or to plunder, because there *remained none* to be the objects of their fury (for they would not have spared *any* had there remained any other such work to be done), Cæsar gave orders that they should demolish the *whole* city and temple, except the western wall of the city, and the three highest towers, Phaselus, Hippicus, and Mariamne; but for all the rest of the wall, it was laid so completely even with the ground, by those who dug it up to the foundation, that there was nothing left to make those who came hither believe that it *was ever inhabited.*" Scott says, "The Roman victors forbade any Jew to dwell in their ancient inheritance, or to come within sight of Jerusalem; the foundations of the old city were ploughed up."

If one will "*rightly* divide the word of truth" he can perceive that by the *Roman* invasion was fulfilled, not the prophecy of Zechariah, but of Micah—" Therefore shall Zion for your sake be *plowed as a field*, and Jerusalem shall become *heaps*, and the mountain of the house as the high places *of the forest.*"—Mic. iii, 12. I believe that the Saviour's feet will as literally and truly stand on the Mount of Olives at His return, verse 4, as they did when He was formerly here. Certainly He literally *ascended* from that mountain, and will so come in like manner.—Ac. i, 11. To say that verse 4 was fulfilled at the Roman invasion by the standing of the feet of *Titus* on the Mount of Olives would be a monstrous torture and perversion of this prophecy. And besides, the great earthquake, rending the mountain and forming a " very great valley " between, did not occur when Titus invaded Jerusalem; it is an undivided mountain to this day, and will remain so till the Lord comes. Notice, too, that no such perennial streams are *now* flowing out east and west from Jerusalem as verse 8 describes; and this also shows the prophecy remains to be accomplished. It proves, too, that the earth will not be blotted out of existence when He comes, for " *summer and winter* " will still go on, during which those two rivers will run, the one to the Mediterranean and the other to the Dead Sea. The going of " all nations " to Jerusalem *once* a year (verse 16) was not fulfilled under the Mosaic dispensation, for that required the Jews *alone* to go thither for worship; and *they* had to go *thrice* a year.—Deut. xvi, 16. Nor does the compelling of all nations to go to Jerusalem to worship, and the withholding of rain from the wicked, apply to the *present* dispensation, for the Lord *now* "sendeth rain on the just and on the unjust" (Mat. v, 45), and no nation is required to go to Jerusalem to worship. These predictions, therefore, *must* belong to a dispensation yet to come, the Millennium, after the advent.

11th. How can the resurrected saints reign

during the Millennium (Rev. xx, 4), unless those two inseparable events—the advent and resurrection—take place *before* it? One of the classes to be raised will be "them that were *beheaded*." Now if the beheading be literal, why not the rising also? If there were any doubt about the literalness of the rising from the dead, that doubt ought to be set aside by the explanation which the Spirit here gives of the vision—" This is the first *resurrection*." I conclude that the word resurrection (*anastasis*) is twice used here in its most literal sense; for, if there be any enigma in the preceding verses, it is certainly not customary to explain an enigma in language that is itself enigmatical, or to explain one figurative expression by another equally figurative. That the first resurrection includes *all* the righteous dead, we learn from other and supplementary portions of Scripture.—1 Cor. xv, 23; 1 Thes. iv, 16. "The resurrection of *the just*" is a "resurrection (*ek nekrōn*) *from among the dead*," as the Greek implies, and hence it is a *first* resurrection, for it leaves other dead remaining in the grave till the end of the Millenium.—Lu. xiv, 14; xx, 35. Those who shall rise first are *firstborns*, prōtotokoi.—Heb. xii, 23. How could the first resurrection be only the reviving of a martyr-like disposition, seeing that Satan will then be bound, and no one left to act the part of persecutor; martyrdom implies severe persecution. Those who talk of such a reviving, basing their notion

11

on the case of Elijah and John, ought to first be able to prove that any inspired writer has ever once declared the coming of John to be the *resurrection* of Elijah. As to the word "souls," the Commentary of Jamieson, Faussett and Brown very truly says, "*Souls* is often used in general for *persons*, and even for *dead bodies.*" In Num. ix, 6, 7, where the English has "*dead body* of a man," the Greek has *psuche anthrōpou*, "*soul* of a man.*" Balaam said, "Let *me* (Greek, *hee psuche mou*, 'the *soul* of me,' margin 'my soul') die the death of the righteous."—Num. xxiii, 10. If then "the soul of me" means "me" in that place, why should not "the souls of them" mean "them" in this place? When we read that "eight *souls*" were saved in the ark, does anybody imagine that their *bodies* were *not* saved? Here let me quote what one or two modern writers have to say as to the manner of interpreting these verses (Rev. xx, 4-6). Bishop Newton, an Episcopalian, born 1704, says, "This prophecy remains to be fulfilled, even though the resurrection be taken only for an *allegory*, which yet the text cannot admit without the greatest *torture and violence.*" Dean Alford, probably the greatest scholar which the Episcopal Church has had in its communion for a long time, says, "Those who lived next to the apostles, and the WHOLE church for THREE HUNDRED YEARS understood these verses in the PLAIN and LITERAL sense.

As regards the text itself, no legitimate treatment of it will extort what is known as the spiritual interpretation now in fashion. If the first resurrection is spiritual, then so is the second, which I suppose none will be hardy enough to maintain; but if the second is *literal*, then so is the *first*, which, in common with the WHOLE PRIMITIVE CHURCH and many of the *best modern* expositors, I do maintain and receive as an article of faith and hope."

12th. To affirm that Christ will not come till the end of the Millennium is daring to affirm that He will not come for a thousand years yet, inasmuch as we know the Millennium has not begun. This putting off the advent a thousand years is contrary to the *watching, waiting and expectant* attitude which Christians are required to maintain. "Watch ye, therefore; for ye know not *when* the Master of the house cometh, at even, or at midnight, or at the cock-crowing, or in the morning; lest *coming suddenly* He find you *sleeping*. Let your loins be *girded about*, and your *lights burning;* and ye yourselves like unto men that *wait for* their Lord, when he will return from the wedding; that when he cometh and knocketh, they may open unto him *immediately*. Blessed are those servants whom the lord when he cometh shall find *watching*."—Mark xiii, 35, 36; Lu. xii, 35, 36, 37.

These twelve overwhelming reasons are but a

fragment of the evidence which might be brought in proof that the personal coming of the Lord Jesus will occur *before* the Millennium. Having proved from Scripture that the advent will take place before the Millennium, allow me, before closing this part of the subject, to glance briefly at the history of this doctrine. Eusebius, born in Palestine about A.D. 270, and who is called "the father of ecclesiastical history," tells us that Papias said, "That there will be a Millennium *after the resurrection* from the dead, when the *personal* reign of Christ will be established on this earth."—Hist. Eccles. iii, 39. Irenæus informs us that Papias was "the hearer of John and a companion of Polycarp."—Against Heresies, B. v, ch. xxxiii, Clark's edition. Those advocating this in modern times are called Premillennarians, and those who think the advent will not occur till *after* the Millennium are called Postmillennarians. On the doctrine of Premillennarians the "Dictionary of Religious Knowledge," by Abbott and Conant, says, "These views may be traced to the earliest history of the church, and were advocated by the fathers up to the 4th century. They then declined, till the Reformation gave them a new impulse, since which time they have prevailed through the entire church to a large extent." Macauley, the historian, in his essay on the Jews, remarks, "The Christian believes, as well as the Jew, that at some future period the present order of things will come to an end. Nay, many Christians believe that the Messiah will shortly establish a kingdom on the earth, and reign visibly over all its inhabitants. The number of people who hold it is very much greater than the number of Jews residing in England. Many of those who hold it are distinguished by rank, wealth and ability. It is preached from the pulpits both of the Scottish and English churches. Noblemen and members of Parliament have written in defence of it. They expect that before this generation shall pass away, all the kingdoms of the earth will be swallowed up in one divine empire." On the 30th and 31st of October and 1st of November, 1878, a great " Prophetic Conference" assembled in New York and agreed on the following among other resolutions :—

" II. The prophetic words of the Old Testament Scriptures, concerning the first coming of our Lord Jesus Christ, were literally fulfilled in His birth, life, death, resurrection and ascension ; and so the prophetic words of both the Old and New Testaments concerning His second coming will be literally fulfilled in His visible bodily return to this earth in like manner as He went up into heaven; and this glorious Epiphany of the great God, and our Saviour Jesus Christ, is the blessed hope of the believer and of the Church during this entire dispensation."

" III. This second coming of the Lord Jesus is

everywhere in the Scriptures represented as *imminent*, and may occur at *any moment;* yet the precise day and hour thereof is unknown to man, and known only to God."

"IV. The Scriptures nowhere teach that the whole world will be converted to God, and that there will be a reign of universal righteousness and peace *before* the return of our blessed Lord."

The conference was composed of prominent members of the following denominations:—Baptist, Congregational, Methodist, Presbyterian and Episcopal.

It is very important to remember that although there will be a very great destruction of the ungodly at the advent, yet mortal nations in a probationary state will exist on earth during the Millennium, and subject to the laws of that dispensation. Thus during the first thousand years after the Lord Jesus takes possession of the earth there will be a glorious fulfillment of the promise made to Abraham—"Thy Seed shall possess the gate of His enemies; and in thy Seed shall all the nations of the earth be blessed."—Gen. xxii, 17, 18. As in the promise, so in its fulfillment, the blessing comes *after* the taking possession of the gate of His enemies i. e. after His conquest of the world. In His sending the Gospel to the Gentiles and taking out of them a people for His name the Seed of Abraham gives an individual foretaste of the national blessedness which the world will enjoy during the *Millennium,* which will be the *grand* fulfillment of that promise. As to the *present* condition of the nations, it has been estimated that about 800,000,000 of people are now bowing down to stocks and stones. There is "a vail that is spread over all nations," both Jews and Gentiles.—Isa. xxv, 7. Darkness covers the earth, and gross darkness the people.—Isa. LX, 2. "The whole world lieth in wickedness."—1 Jno. v, 19. "All nations" are "*deceived*" by Satan and by the sorceries of Babylon.—Rev. xviii, 23. But in the Millennial age, after the fearful judgments of the second advent are over, and Christ has entered upon His peaceful personal reign, this promised blessedness will be realized in its *fullness;* for then Satan shall be bound so "that he shall deceive the nations *no more* till the thousand years shall be be fulfilled." Then "the Gentiles shall come unto the Lord from the *ends of the earth,* and shall say "Surely our fathers have inherited *lies, vanity,* and things wherein there is *no profit.*"—Jer. xvi, 19. Also the Beast and the False Prophet will have been destroyed in the lake of fire.—Rev. xix, 20; xx, 3. And "at that time they shall call Jerusalem the throne of the Lord; and *all the nations* shall be gathered unto it, to the name of the Lord, to Jerusalem; neither shall they walk *any more* after the imagination of their evil heart."— Jer. iii, 17. Yea "*All nations* shall flow unto it. . . . Nation shall not lift up sword against nation;

neither shall they learn war any more."—Isa. ii, 2–4. "Every one that is *left* of all the nations which came against Jerusalem shall even go up from year to year to worship the King, the Lord of hosts, and to keep the feast of tabernacles."— Zec. xiv, 16. "*All people, nations and languages shall serve Him.*"—Dan. vii, 14. "*All nations shall come and worship before*" *Him.*—Rev. xv, 4. Remember, these testimonies are the voice of Scripture; they *must* be fulfilled. And you must confess that when they are fulfilled in the future millennial state of the world "all nations" will indeed be blessed religiously, politically, socially, and even physically, as they have never been blessed before. But of course we are not to suppose that the now deceased heathen will be raised from the dead and allowed to enjoy that probation and blessedness, for *they* died as they lived, "*without hope,*" being "alienated from the life of God through the *ignorance* that was in them." And hence they have no part in "the first resurrection." —Ephes. ii, 12; iv. 18.

The millennial subjugation of *all* nations implies that of the *Jews* also, and the bringing of them under the sceptre of Messiah after their conversion. The title "King of the Jews" is one of the gems treasured up in "the unsearchable riches of Christ," and is destined yet to be worn upon His divine brow, and thence to scintillate its holy light over a subdued and peaceful world. They have now been abiding "many days *without* a king" (Hos. iii, 4, 5), but the Father has declared the Son to be a "Governor that SHALL rule my people Israel."—Mat. ii, 2, 6 ; John i, 49. Their rejection of Him at His *first* is no proof that they will do the same at His *second* coming. They rejected Moses at the *first*, but submitted to him at the *second* time, he being then clothed with power to destroy their enemies. "Thy people shall be *willing* in the day of thy *power*."—Psa. cx, 3. There seems to be a typical meaning in the remarkable fact that "at the *second* time Joseph was made known to his brethren."—Ac. vii, 13. Moses and Joseph were typical of Christ in some things, especially, I think, in this. When they accept the returning Messiah as their King they will indeed have a Governor "from the midst of them," and a King "whom the Lord hath chosen."—Jer. xxx, 21 ; Deut. xvii, 15. Prophecy affords abundant testimony to the future conversion and restoration of Israel. "He that scattered Israel will gather him and keep him, as a shepherd doth his flock."—Jer. xxxi, 10. If this means the literal Israel *scattered* from the literal land, must it not also mean the *literal* Israel *gathered* to the *literal* land ? Their *national* conversion and restoration of course does not mean the eternal salvation of every individual Jew that ever lived. Their *national* deliverance from Egypt was not a deliverance of every individual Jew who had ever died and been buried in Egypt. Concerning the restoration, Micah is very plain and unmistakable. In describing a state of things, which all who are even slightly acquainted with history must admit has never yet obtained, and which belongs only to the glorious days of Messiah's reign, Micah says:—" And he shall judge many people, and rebuke strong nations afar off; and they shall beat their swords into plough-shares and their spears into pruning-hooks; nation shall not lift up sword against nation, neither shall they learn war any more. But they shall sit every man under his vine and under his fig tree, and none shall make them afraid, for the mouth of the Lord of hosts hath spoken it. . . . *In that day,* saith the Lord, will I *assemble* her that is driven out, and her that I have afflicted. And I will make her that halted a remnant, and her that was cast far off a *strong nation,* and the Lord shall reign over them in mount Zion from henceforth even *forever.*"—iv, 3, 4, 6, 7.

Remember that this is the same Micah who a few verses after predicted that our Lord would be born in Bethlehem; and as his Bethlehem is a literal Bethlehem in the land of Judea, so we must conclude that his Zion will be a literal Zion in the same land.

By " her that halted" and " her that is driven out" is meant the Jewish nation, driven out of the land, and " *led away captive into all nations"* for their many sins. But that since their last dispersion they have never been thus assembled and gathered and made a strong nation is evident from their present dispersed and weak condition; and also from the intensely warlike condition of the other nations. For *contemporaneously* or "*in that day*" of Israel's gathering, the rest of mankind, even including "strong nations afar off," shall be rebuked into peace, so that they shall beat their swords into plough-shares and their spears into pruning-hooks, neither will they learn war any more. All the military schools, arsenals, conscriptions, militia, and volunteer companies found among the "strong nations" of the earth, declare as with loud-mouthed artillery tones that such a state of things has *not yet* obtained. Moreover we are bound to conclude that when the nations are thus at peace, and Israel thus restored, the Lord will reign over them in mount Zion just as literally as he was born in Bethlehem.

Whatever partial restoration of Jews to Palestine may have taken place it cannot be the one here spoken of by Micah who is foretelling a *final* restoration and settlement, inasmuch as it is to be "*forever*." That word "forever" puts a stop to their wanderings, and shuts out the idea of any subsequent dispersion, such as that by the Romans in A.D. 70. And since Micah's testimony that "the Lord shall reign over them in mount Zion from henceforth even *forever*" is in almost the exact words of Gabriel's, "He shall reign over the house of Jacob *forever*," the great truth is made to flash upon our minds that both are alluding to the same grand epoch, and describing a state of things *future even at the birth of Christ.*

"Therefore behold the days come, saith the Lord, that they shall no more say the Lord liveth which brought up the children of Israel out of the land of Egypt; but the Lord liveth which brought up, and which led the seed of the house of Israel out of the *north* country, and from *all* countries whither I had driven them; and they shall dwell in their own land." Jer. xxiii, 7, 8; Isa. xi, 11, 12; xliii, 1, 7; xlix, 22, 26; Jer. xxx, 8, 9; xxxi; Hos. iii, 4, 5. This great national restoration under Christ as their King will, as a necessary consequence, be attended with their national *conversion* to Christ. Thus Paul in speaking beyond a doubt of this event, says, "Blindness in part has happened to Israel, until the fullness of the Gentiles be come in." "And so all Israel shall be saved; as it is written. There shall come out of Zion the Delieverer, and shall turn away ungodliness from Jacob."--Rom. xi, 25, 26. "And it shall come to pass in that day that the Lord shall set His hand again the *second* time to recover the remnant of His people which shall be left, from Assyria, and from Egypt, and from Pathros, and from Cush, and from Elam, and from Shinar, and from Hamath, and from the islands of the sea."—Isaiah xi, 11. On this verse the Commentary of Jamieson, Faussett & Brown very truly says, "Therefore the coming restoration of the Jews is to be distinct from that after the Babylonish captivity, and yet to resemble it. The first restoration was *literal*, therefore so shall the second be; the latter, however, it is implied here, shall be much more universal than the former." They will then no longer "abide in unbelief," for the Lord "will give them a heart to know Him;" will "*take away the stony heart*" of unbelief, "put His Spirit within them," and "turn away ungodliness from them." This, plainly enough, accounts for their great national conversion.—Jer. xxiv, 7; Eze. xxxvi, 26, 27; Rom. xi, 26. "Without faith it is impossible to please God" (Heb. xi, 6), but their faith will be largely the result of sight, somewhat after the manner of Thomas who would not believe otherwise. Paul too was converted by *seeing* the Lord Jesus; and that event seems to foreshadow and illustrate the future conversion of his brethren.

Perhaps it may not be a waste of time to glance briefly at what several uninspired writers have said on the subject. Dr. William Jenks, Editor of the "Comprehensive Commentary," says on Rom. xi, 26 :—" The Editor is at a loss to conceive how any attentive reader of the prophecies can come to any other conclusion than that there is yet to be a glorious restoration of the Jews; probably to their own land, certainly to the Church and Gospel privileges; and this has been, as Whitby shows, the constant doctrine of the Church." On Isa. lii, 1, Scott says, "Nothing can be supposed more interesting than the future restoration of Israel to the church and to their own land; no event is more evidently predicted in Scripture." C. H. Spurgeon, the London Baptist preacher, says, " I think we do not attach sufficient importance to the restoration of the Jews. But certainly if there is anything promised in the Bible, it is this. I imagine that you cannot read the Bible without seeing clearly that there is to be an actual restoration of the children of Israel. May that happy day soon come! For when the Jews are restored, then the fullness of the Gentiles shall be gathered in ; and as soon as they return, then shall Jesus come upon mount Zion to reign with His ancients gloriously, and the halcyon days of the Millennium shall then dawn."—Sermon vii, A.D. 1856. Tertullian, about A.D. 200, says:—" At His last coming He will favor with His acceptance and blessing the circumcision also, even the race of Abraham, which by-and-by is to acknowledge Him."—Against Marcion, B. v, c. ix.

If, as some " Adventists" have thought, there is to be no *mortality* during the thousand years, but only an immortal and perfected population on the earth, wherein would that thousand years differ in one single respect from the great and infinite eternity beyond? The fact that it is called "THE *thousand* years" proves it will be a *special* thousand years, differing from all that ever went before it, or that shall ever come after it. (The "light" of that millennial day will not be "clear" like the perfect glory of the great eternity beyond nor "dark" like the present state, but it shall be peculiarly "one day which shall be known to the Lord." The common day is succeeded by darkness, but that millennial day will be succeeded by the *greater splendour* of endless glory, for "at evening time it shall be *light*.") Why should there be mediatorship "after the order of Melchisedec" during the thousand years if no one shall then be living in the mortal state to *need* mediation? And why should leaves be provided " for the *healing* of the nations" if there shall be no nations to need healing?—Rev. xxii, 2. And why bind Satan lest he should "*deceive* the nations" if there shall then be no one in the mortal state *liable* to being deceived? How can there be a rebellion of mortal nations at the *end* of the Millennium if they shall all be blotted out of existence a *thousand years before?*—Rev. xx, 3, 8. Indeed why should the millennial *subjects* of Christ and the saints be called "*the nations*" at all, if they are not still in the mortal state? Surely immortals could not be *punishable by plague and drought* as the "left" of the nations will be if they come not up to Jerusalem to worship.—Zec. xiv, 16–19. Also the memorial *sacrifices* to be offered in that age, indicate the presence of *mortality* still pleading for pardon and reconciliation through the blood of Christ. (Those emblematic sacrifices will commemorate and point to the "*one* sacrifice" on the cross; as the Lord's supper does in the present dispensation.—Zec. xiv, 21 ; Eze. xlv, 15–25.) Believers, gathered out of the present dispensation are "a kind of *first-fruits ;*" does not this imply a *harvest* from the millennial dispensation that is to follow ? and, of course, that harvest will have to be gathered from a *mortal* race.—Jas. i, 18. Probation, with its consequent liability to transgression and death, existed in Eden in the days when the Lord condescended to walk and talk with Adam and Eve. Then why not believe it will exist in the Millennium while Christ and His redeemed are reigning personally on earth ? If the Edenic state closed with the rebellion and expulsion of Adam and Eve who had beheld its wonders, and if thousands of Israelites rebelled and were destroyed after what they had seen in the wilderness, is it unreasonable to believe that some of the *mortal* population will rebel and be destroyed after beholding the wonders of the Millennium?

If the burning of which Peter speaks occurs at the *close* of the thousand years, would it not still be an event pertaining to "the day of the Lord," to the *evening* of that day, inasmuch as "one day is with the Lord as a *thousand years*, and a thousand years as *one* day"? We must not suppose that all things predicted of "the last day" or the "day of the Lord" will take place in twenty-four hours after He comes. One meaning of "day," according to Webster, is "any period of time as distinguished from other time." The Greek word for "day" (*hēmera*) has also that meaning in some places, as "At that *time* (*hēmera*) there was a great persecution."—Ac. viii, 1. "Man's judgment," margin, "day" (Greek, *hēmera*).—1 Cor. iv, 3. The American Bible Union's edition (1866) has the following note on this verse:—" Man's day: namely, the present, in contrast with the coming *day of the Lord.*" Man's day, you know, has been a very *long* one; but I trust it is now " far spent," and that we shall soon behold with joy the glorious day of the Lord. Peter tells us to heed the prophets, and some of the similar expressions in their writings are evidently *figurative*, as, "The Lord maketh the earth *empty*, and maketh it *waste* and turneth it *upside down*. . . The land shall be *utterly emptied* and *utterly spoiled*. . . The earth mourneth and *fadeth away*. . . The curse *devoured* the earth. . . The inhabitants of the earth are *burned* and FEW MEN LEFT."—Isa. xxiv, 1, 3, 4, 6. But for those three last words, one might have thought the prophet meant the literal destruction of the earth and its population; but those words prove that the material globe and some of its inhabitants were to survive those judgments. Verses

13-16 prove the same, for "when *thus* it shall be in the midst of the land among the people, there shall be as the shaking of an olive, and as the gleaning grapes when the vintage is done." Heavens and earth often denote those *in* and those *under* authority. Thus Moses when speaking " in the ears of *all* the congregation—both *princes* and *people*— said, " Give ear, O ye *heavens*, and I will speak ; and hear, O *earth*, the words of my mouth."— Deut. xxxi, 30; xxxii, 1. Hence also persons differing in degree of authority are called sun, moon and stars.—Gen. xxxvii, 5-10. If Peter's words be taken figuratively they denote the passing away of all human *governments* " with a great noise " of out-poured wrath on the wicked; after which a new and heavenly order of things will be introduced. But if they be taken literally they denote rather the regeneration or renewal than the annihilation of the material globe, for after the conflagration it is still called " *earth* " (2 Pet iii, 13), and the covenants of promise plainly enough indicate that, in its glorified state, it is to be the perpetual inheritance of the righteous.* As " a

---

* "The general tenor of prophecy, and the analogy of the divine dealings point unmistakeably to *this earth, purified and renewed*, as the eternal habitation of the blessed."— Alford on Mat. v, 12. "Many of the old theologians thought that the whole existing physical universe was to be destroyed. This view is now universally discarded."—" Systematic Theology," by Prof. Hodge, Princeton. " The Bible begins

new (kainē) creature" does not mean *another* creature but only the same, changed for the better; so "a new (kainē) earth" does not mean *another* earth but the same, renewed.

At the close of the Millennium, when the *mortal* nature, shall have disappeared, the kingdom will be delivered up to the Father.—1 Cor. xv, 24. Sin and death having ceased, *Mediatorship* will be a vacated office because the work of reconciliation will be *perfected* and *completed;* and the breach between man and his Creator thoroughly repaired. Hence the *delivering up* denotes that "subjection" or subordination to the Father implied in the cessation of Mediatorship. The Father will then come into a more *direct* connexion with the earth than He had done while the Mediatorial office was existing. Transgressors will have been "rooted out" of the earth, and "*the perfect*" alone left remaining on it.—Prov. ii, 21, 22. Thus will be

with the generations of the heavens and earth; but the Christian revelation ends with the *regenerations,* or new creation of the heavens and the earth. . . The present earth is not to be annihilated."—A. Campbell, in "Ch. System." p. 304, A.D. 1839. "It is more reasonable and philosophical to conclude that the earth shall be *refined* and *restored,* than finally destroyed."—Adam Clarke. Arguing from the upward progression of creative acts in the past, Hugh Miller, the celebrated geologist, says, "We must regard the expectation of 'new heavens and a new earth wherein dwelleth righteousness,' as not unphilosophic, but as, on the contrary, altogether rational and according to experience."—Testimony of the Rocks.—Lec. v.

fully realized the Saviour's prayer, not that His people should be taken *out of* the world, but kept from the *evil*.—Jno. xvii, 15. Then earth and heaven will, as it were, be turned into one; for the will of God shall thenceforth be done in earth " *as it is in heaven* " i. e. perfectly, absolutely, and throughout its whole extent by a glorified population of sinless and immortal beings made in bodily constitution " equal to the angels" and "partakers of the *divine* nature." Such will be the endless and blissful state *beyond* the Millennium. The delivering up of the kingdom is therefore merely a change in the *manner* of its administration, but not an end of the kingdom itself, for it shall have " no end."—Lu. i, 32, 33; Dan. vii, 14; Psa. lxxxix, 29, 36, 37. If allowed to conjecture we might suppose that perhaps the vast harvest of immortalized ones gathered out of the millennial dispensation will be placed under the eternal sovereignty of the Lord Jesus and His *pre*-millennial saints. (There seem to be *degrees* of authority among the angels, as indicated by the title archangel i. e. chief angel). Be this as it may, all who are accounted worthy to inherit the kingdom, in whatever capacity, will enjoy an endless life of unspeakable glory and happiness. Will you come to the Saviour that you may inherit that kingdom and that life? He says, " Him that cometh to me, I will in no wise cast out."—Jno. vi, 37. See an instance in one of His miracles. The great quietude of the ancient Sabbath day had come over the populous town of Capernaum. In the synagogue that day the Lord Jesus had wrought a miracle, and the fame of it had spread from house to house till the city was thrilled with excitement. The other afflicted, hearing with joy that the great Prophet of Israel was in the city, wanted to go or be carried to Him that they too might be healed. But the Pharisees had persuaded them that it was not lawful even to be healed on the Sabbath. So they waited till sun-set, when the Sabbath closed, having begun at sun-set of the previous day. How anxiously those afflicted ones, tossing on beds of pain, must have looked out of the windows to see if the sun was *nearly down!* In one house perhaps it was a beloved son or daughter almost delirious with a burning fever, in another, an aged mother or father paralytic for years—all beseeching their friends to help them to see the Saviour before His departure from the city. And when, in the beautiful twilight, they came and gathered about the door, " He laid his hands on *every one* of them, and healed them;" *none* were slighted. . What a joyful night was that! Some, perhaps, eating the first mouthful that they had relished for weeks; others, cured of lameness, walking and praising God; others, restored to their right mind, conversing with circles of wondering and delighted friends. It is the same Jesus who offers to cure you of *sin* and give you *eternal* life at last. Then why not, without waiting for another sun-set, apply *at once* to so great a Physician? Naaman was told to "wash, and be clean." Will you too, poor sinner, wash and be clean from the leprosy of sin. "Be baptized and wash away thy sins, calling on the name of the Lord." Hear the poor Greek woman crying to the Saviour for the mere "crumbs" of mercy; that her daughter may be healed. With humility and faith she falls down at His feet, saying, "*Lord help me;*" and at once He speaks the healing word. Then how gladly she rises up and hurries home, where, if she had other children, I can imagine they must have come running to meet her, throwing up their little white hands and shouting "O mother! mother! sister is well! sister is well!" On a special occasion the Saviour was teaching the people, "and the power of the Lord was present to heal them;" and His power is here to-day—THE GOSPEL is "the POWER OF GOD unto salvation to every one that believeth."—Rom. i, 16. It has a regenerative power, for "of His own will begat He us by the WORD OF TRUTH . . . and this is the word which by THE GOSPEL is preached unto you."—Jas. i, 18; 1 Pet. i, 23, 25. Hence it is called in another place "the word of truth, the gospel of your *salvation.*"—Ephes. i, 13. The regenerative process is threefold—mental, moral, and physical: "first the blade, then the ear, after that the full corn in the ear."—Mark iv, 28. The *mental* and *moral* parts of the process consist in *believing* and *obeying* THE GOSPEL OF THE KINGDOM; the *physical* part, in being born of the Spirit at the resurrection. Unless you submit to the two first, you can never hope to experience the *third* and *completing* part of this process. Then why not, *at once*, believe and obey the gospel of the kingdom? "The time is short;" if the Lord come not very soon, death will; for the longest human life is brief, compared to eternity. When the dread summons of death arrives, the plow, axe, hammer, yardstick, needle, pen, and all such implements *must* be laid aside; and then, may be, when too late, you will want to talk of the great *hereafter*. Ah! I can imagine a house of mourning from which the family physician has turned away in despair, for none but *Jesus and the resurrection* can help the sufferer now. Enter the sick room. Some persons are leaning against the wall, weeping; others are walking about with hushed voices and softened tread, and eyes filled with tears that will not be suppressed. Draw near the bedside! Do you know the sufferer? Yes, for though much changed by illness, yet some of the features remain—it is *one of you* that are listening to the gospel-invitation to-day! And shall it be well with you in that hour; no remorse and terror, but all calm and peaceful resignation? It depends on the life that you live. O then, I beseech you to begin this day, to live a *Christian life*.

INDEX.

[*Corrigenda:*—p. 9, in some copies, for aleniated read alienated; p. 22, for tiding read tidings; p. 45, for requirements read requirement; p. 134, for Im read I'm; p. 183, for with read worth; p. 206, for is is read is.]

FIRST DISCOURSE:—HOW TO STUDY THE BIBLE	5
SECOND DISCOURSE:—WHAT MUST I DO TO BE SAVED?	28
THIRD DISCOURSE:—THE PROMISES MADE UNTO THE FATHERS; OR, THE COVENANT WITH ABRAHAM	52
FOURTH DISCOURSE:—THE SURE MERCIES; OR, THE COVENANT WITH DAVID	76
FIFTH DISCOURSE:—THE ETERNAL INHERITANCE	98
SIXTH DISCOURSE:—IMMORTALITY, AND HOW IT MAY BE OBTAINED	121
SEVENTH DISCOURSE:—THE SUBJECTS, NATURE, DESIGN AND IMPORTANCE OF CHRISTIAN BAPTISM	157
EIGHTH DISCOURSE:—CHRISTIAN DUTIES AND GRACES TO BE OBSERVED AND CULTIVATED AFTER BAPTISM.	178
NINTH DISCOURSE:—THE KINGDOM AS DISTINGUISHED FROM THE CHURCH. A FEW PROMINENT SIGNS THAT THE KINGDOM IS NEAR	195
TENTH DISCOURSE:—THE SECOND ADVENT, THE MILLENNIUM AND THE STATE BEYOND	223

www.ingramcontent.com/pod-product-compliance
Lightning Source LLC
Chambersburg PA
CBHW032144230426
43672CB00011B/2448